# *Far from Home*

# Far from Home

## Reading and Word Study

SECOND EDITION

# WILLIAM P. PICKETT

Montclair State College
Passaic High School

HEINLE & HEINLE PUBLISHERS

*A Division of Wadsworth, Inc.*
*Boston, Massachusetts 02116*

The publication of *Far from Home: Reading and Word Study,* Second Edition, was directed by the members of the Newbury House Publishing Team at Heinle & Heinle:

Erik Gundersen, Editorial Director
Susan Mraz, Marketing Director
Gabrielle B. McDonald, Production Editor

Also participating in the publication of this program were:

Publisher: Stanley J. Galek
Editorial Production Manager: Elizabeth Holthaus
Project Manager: Cindy Funkhouser
Associate Editor: Lynne Telson Barsky
Associate Marketing Manager: Donna Hamilton
Production Assistant: Maryellen Eschmann
Manufacturing Coordinator: Mary Beth Lynch
Illustrator: Anne Sibley O'Brien
Interior Designer: Greta D. Sibley
Cover Illustrator and Designer: Cynthia Jabar

Far from Home, Second Edition

Manufactured in the United States of America

Library of Congress Cataloging-in-Publication Data

Pickett, William P.,
     Far from home : reading and word study / William P. Pickett. —
2nd ed.
     p.     cm.
     ISBN 0-8384-4852-6
     1. English language—Textbooks for foreign speakers.
2. Vocabulary. 3. Readers. I. Title.
PE1128.P48  1993
428.6'4—dc20                                      93-25537
                                                        CIP


ISBN: 0-8384-4852-6

10 9 8 7 6 5 4

To My Son Edward

# Contents

# *Preface*

## PURPOSE

*Far from Home* is a reading text that emphasizes word study. This book helps students acquire a basic vocabulary that will make them better readers and it accomplishes this end through the presentation of reading as well as other exercises designed to foster the development of a host of language, thinking, and study skills.

## LEVEL

*Far from Home* is for advanced beginning to low intermediate students of English as a second or foreign language. It presumes its readers know the most basic structures of English and its most common words. It presumes they know words like *wait, close, stop, chair,* and *beautiful,* and it teaches words like *share, trust, waste, struggle, reach, neighbor, instead,* and *however.*

## ARTICULATION WITH *AT HOME IN TWO LANDS*

*Far from Home* provides an excellent foundation for the readings and exercises included in *At Home in Two Lands*, an intermediate level reading and vocabulary text by the same author. Though *At Home in Two Lands* has been designed to reinforce and expand the material in *Far from Home*, both texts can be used effectively on their own.

## CONTENT AND FORMAT

### Lead Story

*Far from Home* is divided into six units, each unit with three chapters. Every chapter begins with a picture and preview questions to stimulate students' curiosity and to activate their prior knowledge of the topics in the lead stories.

The lead stories at the beginning of each chapter describe the everyday problems and progress, hopes, and fears of individuals or couples with roots in a variety of cultures and countries. The three lead stories in each unit are about the same person or couple.

The stories are followed by **Comprehension Questions**, some of which go beyond the facts of the story and require the reader to infer and make judgments.

## Word Guessing and Mini-Dictionaries

A **Word Guessing** section comes before the **Mini-Dictionaries**. It gives the student practice in guessing the meaning of a word from the context of the sentence and the story it is in. This should help students develop a very important skill.

The **Mini-Dictionaries** provide brief, clear definitions of the eight key words in the lead story. More important, the **Mini-Dictionaries** give example sentences showing how the key words are actually used. These sections are followed by sentence-completion exercises to test, reinforce, and increase a reader's knowledge of the key words. Next comes a **Creating Sentences** section to foster an independent use of the key words.

## Story Completion and Sharing Information

**Story Completion** includes preview questions and a story that the reader must complete with the key words. After this cloze exercise comes **Sharing Information**, in which the key words serve as a springboard for discussion. This section gives the readers an opportunity to express their ideas and feelings and to improve their oral skills.

## Word Families and Building Words with Prefixes and Suffixes

The **Word Families** section presents the more common words that are derived from the key words, or in a few cases, the words from which the key words have been derived. Finally, **Building Words** explains and studies a common prefix or suffix used to create new words.

## Review Exercises

At the end of each unit are exercises that review and reinforce the 24 key words of the unit. In addition, many of the words taught in earlier lessons are recycled in the stories and exercises of subsequent lessons.

## Additional Material

A map-reading exercise or exercises in reading car ads, help-wanted ads, and real estate ads are included just before the review exercises of Units I, II, III, and IV. This content-based material relates directly to a theme of the unit and the problems of the people in it.

# CHANGES IN THE SECOND EDITION

The second edition of *Far from Home* has a number of changes, and most of them have been mentioned. Preview questions are put before the lead stories, and all of the lead stories are longer to make them more interesting and to provide more reading. The inference questions and **Word Guessing** and **Creating Sentences** sections are new.

The **Mini-Dictionaries** now contain model sentences, and the sentence-completion exercises following the **Mini-Dictionaries** are fewer and more challenging. There are preview questions before the cloze exercises, and these exercises are longer. In the second edition, the sentences in **Word Families** must be completed by the readers. The sentence-completion exercises that came before the cloze exercise in the first edition have been lengthened, changed into chapter tests, and placed in the Teacher's Guide.

# WORD SELECTION

The key words chosen for intensive study in *Far from Home* are high-frequency words or high-frequency idioms. Their frequency was checked with the help of the following books: *The Teacher's Word Book of 30,000 Words* by Thorndike and Lorge; *A General Service List of English Words* by Michael West; *The American Heritage Word Frequency Book* by Carroll, Davies, and Richmann; and *3,000 Instant Words* by Sakiey and Fry.

With a few exceptions, all the key words studied in *Far from Home* are listed among the 3,000 most commonly occurring words in English, according to the Thorndike-Lorge or Sakiey-Fry lists. Low-frequency words like *homesick* and *snore* are defined in footnotes. Idioms are not covered in the lists consulted, but *Far from Home* has only a few, and they are clearly ones of high frequency, for example, *have to, used to,* and *at least.*

# TEACHER'S GUIDE TO THE SECOND EDITION

The Teacher's Guide contains an answer key to all the exercises. Also included are chapter tests and transparency masters of the chapter-opening illustrations.

# ACKNOWLEDGMENTS

I wish to thank Erik Gundersen, Susan Maguire, Lynne Telson Barsky, and Gabrielle B. McDonald of Heinle & Heinle for their encouragement and help in writing the second edition of *Far from Home*. I am also grateful to Kathy Smith, the copyeditor, and to Cindy Funkhouser, the project manager, for their able assistance.

Above all, I thank my wife, Dorothy, for reading all the stories and exercises and helping me improve them.

# Pronunciation Key

To show the pronunciation of a word, most English dictionaries use symbols that are as close as possible to English spelling. The **Mini-Dictionary** section of *Far from Home* also uses these symbols. They are listed below with example words that have the sound the symbols represent.

The best way to learn to pronounce words is to listen to the pronunciation of native speakers and imitate them. The **Mini-Dictionary** provides pronunciation symbols because students frequently do not have the help of native speakers.

## Vowel Sounds

| | | |
|---|---|---|
| a | at, bad | short *a* |
| ā | āge, lāte | long *a* |
| â(r) | câre, bâre | |
| ä | äre, fäther | |
| e | egg, bed | short *e* |
| ē | ēven, wē | long *e* |
| i | it, sick | short *i* |
| ī | īce, līfe | long *i* |
| o | on, hot | short *o* |
| ō | ōpen, gō | long *o* |
| ô | ôff, dôg | |
| oo | book, good | |
| o͞o | to͞o, fo͞od | |
| u | up, bus | short *u* |
| ū* | ūse, mūsic | long *u* |
| û(r) | tûrn, hûrt | |
| oi | voice, noise | |
| ou | out, house | |

| | | |
|---|---|---|
| ə | about (ə·bout´) | ə is a special symbol that indicates a reduced *a*, |
| | elephant (el´ə·fənt) | *e, i, o,* or *u.* English frequently reduces vowel |
| | positive (poz´ə·tiv) | sounds that are not stressed. A reduced vowel |
| | today (tə·dā´) | sound is called a **schwa.** |
| | industry (in´dəs·trē) | |

*yo͞o is also a symbol for long *u.*

xii

## Consonant Sounds

| | | | | |
|---|---|---|---|---|
| b | box, cab | | p | pay, stop |
| ch | child, watch | | r | run, dear |
| d | day, sad | | s | sit, this |
| f | five, self | | sh | shut, brush |
| g | give, bag | | t | ten, but |
| h | hat | | th | thin, teeth |
| j | job | | *th* | *th*e, clo*th*e |
| k | kiss, week | | v | vote, have |
| l | let, bill | | w | want, grow |
| m | man, room | | y | yes |
| n | not, sun | | z | zone, buzz |
| ng | sing | | zh | vision, garage |

# UNIT ONE

# A Young Woman

# CHAPTER ONE
# *Far from Home*

? ? ? ? ? ? ? ? ? ? ? ? ? ? ? ? ? ? ? ? ? ? ? ? ?

# PREVIEW QUESTIONS

**Discuss or think about these questions before reading the story.**

1. Where is San Diego?  Where is Boston?  How far is it from San Diego to Boston?

2. Sometimes an unmarried son or daughter has to leave home to take a job.  How do parents usually feel about this?

3. Why is moving away from home to take a job often good for a young man or woman?

# Far from Home

Tomiko is an accountant and works for a large insurance company in Boston. She's the youngest of three children and has two older brothers. Tomiko was born and lived in San Diego, California, which is **far** from Boston. Her parents are from Japan.

This is Tomiko's first job, and she phones her parents every Sunday. She **misses** them and they miss her. She's their "baby" and they think she's **too** young to live alone, but she laughs at that idea. She's 23 and graduated from college last year. She tells them that she's happy and everything will be fine.

Tomiko **has to** be at work by 8:00. She goes to work by bus because she doesn't like to drive in Boston traffic, and it's too far to walk. After Tomiko leaves her apartment, she **hurries** to the corner to get the bus. If she misses it, she has to wait 20 minutes for the next one and gets to work late.

Tomiko is a good worker, and her employers are happy that they hired her. She's serious about her job and never **wastes** time. At 12:00 she eats a **quick** lunch and is back at her desk by 12:30. She stops work at 4:00. She's tired by then and is happy to go home and relax.

She gets home **around** 5:00, changes her clothes, reads her mail, and listens to music. "I like all kinds of music," she says, "but country music is my favorite." At 5:30 she cooks dinner. She doesn't like to cook, but she has to since she lives alone and doesn't want to eat out. She usually watches the 6:00 news as she eats dinner.

## I.   COMPREHENSION QUESTIONS

**Answer these questions about the story.** *Use your judgment to answer questions with an asterisk(\*). Work in pairs or small groups. The numbers in parentheses show which paragraph in the story has the answer.*

1. Where was Tomiko born?  (1)
2. What country are her parents from?  (1)
*3. Do you think Tomiko can speak Japanese?
*4. She's 23. Why do her parents call her their "baby"?
5. How do her parents feel about her living alone?  (2)
6. Why does she go to work by bus?  (3)
7. What happens if she misses her bus?  (3)
*8. Why does she have to be careful not to be late for work?
9. Why are her employers happy they hired her?  (4)

10. How much time does she take for lunch? (4)
11. What does she do when she gets home? (5)
12. What kind of music does she like the most? (5)

# II. WORD GUESSING

**Guess the meaning of the key words in these sentences.** *Use the context of the story and the sentences to guess. Circle your answers.*

1. Tomiko was born and lived in San Diego, California, which is **far** from Boston.

   a. bigger than
   b. very different from
   c. warmer than
   d. a great distance from

2. At 12:00 Tomiko eats a **quick** lunch and is back at her desk by 12:30.

   a. big
   b. hot
   c. fast
   d. small

3. Tomiko is serious about her job and never **wastes** *time*.

   a. looks at her watch
   b. uses time poorly
   c. helps others
   d. works slowly

# III. MINI-DICTIONARY — PART ONE

## *Vocabulary Focus*

1. **far** (fär)    *adverb:* at or to a great distance
   *adjective:* distant

   "Tokyo is **far** from New York City."

   "Carmen is swimming to the **far** side of the river."

2. **miss** (mis)    *verb:* A. not to hit, catch, or meet something or someone; not to be present

   B. to feel bad because a person or thing you love is not present

   *noun:* the act of not hitting, catching, or meeting; absence

   "Frank doesn't want to **miss** the dance, but he's working tonight."

   "My wife is in the hospital. The children and I **miss** her."

   "Phil is playing baseball. He missed the first two pitches. Another **miss** and he's out."

3. **too** (t$\overline{oo}$)   *adverb:* more than is good or necessary*

   "This shirt is **too** small.  I need a bigger one."

   *Another common meaning of **too** is *also*.  "Gary is going to the park, and I want to go, **too**."

4. **have to** (hav t$\overline{oo}$ *or* haf´tə)  **has to** (haz t$\overline{oo}$ *or* has´tə)

   *idiom:*  to be necessary; must

   "I **have to** clean my room.  It's dirty."

## Completing Sentences

**Complete the sentences with these words.**  *Use each word twice.  Where a word has different endings, both forms are given.*

| far | misses/missed | too | have to/has to |
| --- | --- | --- | --- |

1. Mark can't do the math problems.  They're _____ hard for him.

2. Juan came to the United States last month.  He _____ his country

   and friends.

3. Paula _____ take the baby to the doctor for a checkup.

4. Do we have _____ to go before we get to our motel?  I'm tired.

5. I'm not going to buy these shoes.  They cost _____ much.

6. You can drive to the beach in five minutes.  It's not _____ .

7. Monica _____ class yesterday.  She was sick.

8. I'm going to get home very late.  I _____ phone my wife.

## Creating Sentences

**Write an original sentence using these words.**  *Work with a partner or on your own.*

1. (far) _____

   _____

2. (miss) _____

   _____

3. (too)_____

_____

4. (have to)_____

_____

# IV. MINI-DICTIONARY — PART TWO

## *Vocabulary Focus*

5. **hur·ry** (hûr´ē)  *verb:* to move fast

   *noun:* the act of moving fast

   "Don is 80 and likes to work slowly.  He doesn't like to **hurry**."

   "Jennifer called the police and they came in a **hurry**."

6. **waste** (wāst)  *verb:* to spend or use poorly; not to use

   *noun:* poor use of something

   "I don't like to **waste** food.  I eat everything on my plate."

   "We don't learn anything in that class.  It's a **waste** of time."

7. **quick** (kwik)  *adjective:* fast

   "The problem is serious.  We must take **quick** action."

8. **a·round** (ə-round´)  *preposition:* about; near in number or time*

   "There were **around** 40 people at the party."

   ***Around** has other meanings.  For example, it means *on all sides of.*  "They put a fence **around** their yard."

## *Completing Sentences*

**Complete the sentences with these words.**  *Use each word twice.  Where a word has different endings, both forms are given.*

| around | hurry/hurrying | quick | wasting/wasted |
| --- | --- | --- | --- |

1. Hakeem _____ an hour waiting in line for tickets to the concert.

   There were none left.

2. It's _____ five miles from Cindy's house to the ocean.

3. Do we have time for a _____ drink?

4. Brian is _____ to the meeting. He doesn't want to be late.

5. The book is _____ 400 pages long.

6. No one is using those lights. Turn them off. We're _____ energy.

7. What's your _____? It's 6:30 and the play doesn't begin until 8:00.

8. I'm going to take a _____ shower before we eat.

## Creating Sentences

**Write an original sentence using these words.** *Work with a partner or on your own.*

5. (hurry) _____

_____

6. (waste) _____

_____

7. (quick) _____

_____

8. (around) _____

_____

# V. STORY COMPLETION

**Discuss or think about these questions before completing the story that follows.**

1. Why is candy bad for our teeth?
2. Why is it important to floss* our teeth?
3. How often should a person go to the dentist for a checkup? Why?
   *To **floss** is *to clean between one's teeth with a thin thread.*

Complete the story with these words.

has to          waste          too          around

missed          far           quick          hurry

## A Bad Toothache

Megan is careful to brush her teeth twice a day and to floss them at night, but she has many problems with them. The difficulty is that she eats _____ much candy and doesn't go to the dentist for regular checkups.

She _____ work today because she has a bad toothache. She is going to the dentist this afternoon.

It's _____ 12:40 now, and Megan is eating a _____ lunch. She _____ be at the dentist's office by 1:00. It's not _____ to the dentist's office, but she'll have to _____ to get there on time. She doesn't have a minute to _____ .

# VI.   SHARING INFORMATION

**Discuss these questions and topics in pairs or small groups.**

1. Do your parents live **far** from you? Where do they live?

2. Where were you born? Where did you grow up? If you moved from there, whom do you **miss**? What do you miss?

3. Complete one of the following sentences. I _____ **too** much. I _____ **too** much _____ .

4. Name something that you **have to** do today or tomorrow.

5. Many visitors from other countries think that people in the United States are always **hurrying**. What do you think?

6. Give some examples of how people **waste** time, food, money, or energy.

7. Some people work **quickly**; others work slowly. They take their time. Do you like to work quickly, or do you like to take your time?

8. Complete the following sentences. I usually eat dinner **around** _____.

   A new shirt costs **around** _____.

# VII.   WORD FAMILIES

**Complete the sentences with these words.** *If necessary, add an ending to the word so it forms a correct sentence.* (adj. = adjective and adv. = adverb)

1. **miss** (verb or noun)          **missing** (adj.)

   A. I looked everywhere for the _____ check.

   B. Harry was in Europe for a week and we _____ him.

2. **waste** (verb or noun)          **wasteful** (adj.)

   A. Don't _____ your time talking to Pete. He won't change.

   B. It's _____ to leave the car running while you're waiting for your

   child to come out of school.

3. **quick** (adj.)          **quickly** (adv.)          **quickness** (noun)

   A. The secretary typed the letter _____ .

   B. Sally does everything fast. She's known for her _____.

   C. Fernando took a _____ look at the menu and ordered a

   hamburger.

# VIII.  BUILDING ADVERBS WITH -LY

An adjective is a word that goes with a noun and tells us something about it.  "It's a **clear** day."  An adverb is a word that goes with a verb or adjective.  "Matthew writes **clearly**."

The ending or suffix **-ly** is added to many adjectives to form an adverb.  For example, *clear + ly = clearly;  quick + ly = quickly.*

When **-ly** is added to an adjective, it usually means *in a certain way.*  For example, *clearly* means *in a clear way;  quickly* means *in a quick way.*

| Adjective | Adverb | | Adjective | Adverb |
| --- | --- | --- | --- | --- |
| careful | carefully | | quick | quickly |
| clear | clearly | | safe | safely |
| easy | easily | | slow | slowly |
| free | freely | | soft | softly |
| glad | gladly | | strong | strongly |
| happy | happily | | usual | usually |
| nice | nicely | | warm | warmly |
| poor | poorly | | | |

**Use the adjectives and adverbs in parentheses to complete these sentences.**

1. It was _____ to fix the TV.  I fixed it _____.

   (easy/easily)

2. Nancy thinks _____ .  She's a _____ thinker.

   (quick/quickly)

3. These children are _____ .  Look how _____ they

   are playing.  (nice/nicely)

4. Angelo is a _____ driver.  He drives _____ .

   (careful/carefully)

5. It's cold outside! Dress _____! Your _____ coat is

   in the closet.  (warm/warmly)

6. Joy has a _____ voice.  She speaks _____.

   (soft/softly)

7. Jim and Jean are _____ married.  They have a _____

   marriage.  (happy/happily)

8. Stan is a _____ worker.  He works _____.

   (slow/slowly)

# CHAPTER TWO
# *A Dog and a Boyfriend*

## ? ? ? ? ? ? ? ? ? ? ? ? ? ? ? ? ? ? ? ? ? ? ? ?

## PREVIEW QUESTIONS

**Discuss or think about these questions before reading the story.**

1. What are some of the problems of living alone in a big city like Boston?
2. Do you think that there is more stealing today than in the past?
3. Is there more stealing in the United States than in other countries?  If so, why?
4. Why do people have dogs?

# A Dog and a Boyfriend

Tomiko likes Boston.  There are many interesting places to go and **a lot of** things to do, but it's not easy to live alone in a big city far from home.  Tomiko never tells her parents, but sometimes she gets a little homesick,[1] and she often feels **afraid** at night.  That's why she has three locks on her apartment door and **owns** a large dog.

The dog is a German shepherd named King.  He's good company and he protects Tomiko.  He also **protects** her apartment when she's at work.  King is friendly if he knows you.  **However**, he barks[2] at people he doesn't know.  Most people are afraid of King when they hear him bark or see how big he is.

Tomiko has a boyfriend named Ted.  He works in the same company as Tomiko, and he's also an accountant.  He's very nice, but there's one problem.  He's afraid of dogs.

The other night Ted came to visit Tomiko.  She said to him, "Don't be afraid of King.  He won't **bite**."  However, Ted doesn't **trust** King.  He's too big and barks too much.  Ted's afraid King **may** bite him.

Ted takes Tomiko out to dinner every Saturday night.  Her favorite restaurant is Anthony's Pier, which has the best fish in Boston and a nice view of the harbor.  After they eat, they go dancing.  Tomiko loves to dance and she's a great dancer.  Ted likes to dance, too, but he's not as good as Tomiko.

Ted is crazy about[3] Tomiko and wants to marry her.  But he knows it's too soon to ask.  She likes him **a lot** and her love for him is growing, but she isn't thinking of marrying him.  However, some day she may.  He's the nicest boyfriend she's ever had.

---

[1] **To be homesick** is *to feel sad (or "sick") because you are away from home.*
[2] **A bark** is *the sound a dog makes.* **To bark** is *to make this sound.*
[3] **To be crazy about** is *to love very much.*

# I.  COMPREHENSION QUESTIONS

## *True or False*

**If the sentence is true, write T.  If it's false, write F and change it to a true statement.**
*Number 1 is done as an example.*

___F___  1. Tomiko tells her parents that she's homesick.

(She never tells them she's homesick.)

_____ 2. It would be difficult to break into her apartment.

_____

_____ 3. Most people trust King.

_____

_____ 4. Ted works in the same company as Tomiko.

_____

_____ 5. He's afraid King may bite him.

_____

_____ 6. He's a better dancer than Tomiko.

_____

_____ 7. He loves Tomiko so much he wants to marry her.

_____

_____ 8. She wants to marry him.

_____

## What Do You Think?

**Use your experience, judgment, and the story to answer these questions.** *The story alone won't answer them.*

1. Do you think Tomiko goes out alone at night? Explain your answer.
2. Does King know that Ted is afraid of him? Explain your answer.
3. Tomiko and Ted are accountants. They like to eat out and dance. They have common interests. How important are common interests in making and keeping friendships?
4. Do you think Ted will marry Tomiko? Explain your answer.

# II.  WORD GUESSING

**Guess the meaning of the key words in these sentences.** *Use the context of the story and the sentences to guess.  Circle your answers.*

1. There are many interesting places to go and **a lot of** things to do.

    a. educational

    b. many

    c. interesting

    d. great

2. Tomiko feels **afraid** at night.  That's why she has three locks on her apartment door.

    a. tired

    b. sad

    c. hungry

    d. scared

3. King is good company and he **protects** Tomiko.

    a. loves

    b. plays with

    c. defends

    d. understands

# III.  MINI-DICTIONARY — PART ONE

## *Vocabulary Focus*

1. **a lot of, a lot** (ə lot əv *or* ə-lot´ə)
    *idiom:* a large quantity or number; much
    "Louise has **a lot of** money in the bank.  She's rich."
    "Roy studies **a lot** and does well in school."

2. **a·fraid** (of) (ə-frād´)  *adjective:* feeling fear; nervous
    "Chris is **afraid** of his boss."

3. **own** (ōn)  *verb:* to have; to possess
    *adjective:* belonging to oneself
    "Gloria and Manuel **own** a beautiful home."
    "Anne has her **own** business."

4. **pro·tect** (prə-tekt´)  *verb:* to defend
    "In the summer, I wear sunglasses to **protect** my eyes."

15

## Completing Sentences

**Complete the sentences with these words.** *Use each word twice. Where a word has different endings, both forms are given.*

own/owns          protect/protects          afraid          a lot of/a lot

1. The little boy is _____ of the dark.

2. Alan lives in the country and _____ a large farm.

3. The Secret Service _____ the president at all times.

4. Lenny drinks _____ water in the summer when the weather is hot.

5. My daughter is 17 and has her _____ phone.

6. When Joy comes home late at night, she's _____ .

7. Ernie knows _____ about the city; he's a taxi driver.

8. Regina is careful to lock the doors at night to _____ herself and her family.

## Creating Sentences

**Write an original sentence using these words.** *Work with a partner or on your own.*

1. (a lot of) _____

   _____

2. (afraid) _____

   _____

3. (own) _____

   _____

4. (protect) _____

   _____

# IV. MINI-DICTIONARY — PART TWO

## Vocabulary Focus

5. **how·ev·er** (hou-ev´ər) *conjunction:* but*

   "Nicole drives very fast. **However**, she's never had an accident."

   ***But** and **however** are close in meaning. **But** is used more often than **however**, especially in conversation. **However** is more formal than **but**.

6. **bite** (bīt) *verb:* to put one's teeth into

   *noun:* the act or result of biting

   "Vicky is **biting** an apple."

   "Min Ho took a **bite** of the cake, but he didn't like it."

   The past of **bite** is **bit**.

7. **trust** (trust) *verb:* to feel that a person is honest and wants to help, or that a thing works well

   *noun:* a feeling that a person is honest and wants to help, or that a thing works well

   "I **trust** Dave. He's nice and likes to help people."

   "Arlene is a good friend of mine. There's a lot of **trust** between us."

8. **may** (mā) *verb:* to be possible; to be uncertain*

   "We **may** go to the movies tonight. We're not sure yet."

   ***May** is also used to ask for permission to do something. "**May** I use your phone, please?"

## Completing Sentences

**Complete the sentences with these words.** *Use each word twice. Where a word has different endings, both forms are given.*

| trust/trusts | however | may | bite/bites |
| --- | --- | --- | --- |

1. My sister and brother-in-law _____ come to see us Sunday afternoon.

2. The bicycle cost a lot; _____, I bought it.

3. When the baby gets angry, he _____ .

4. I travel a lot. I need a car I can _____ .

17

5. Eddie and Timmy have a bad habit. They _____ their fingernails.

6. Our refrigerator is 18 years old. We _____ need a new one soon.

7. Diane has known me for many years. She _____ me.

8. The sky is clear now. _____ , it's going to rain tomorrow.

## Creating Sentences

**Write an original sentence using these words.** *Work with a partner or on your own.*

5. (however) _____

_____

6. (bite) _____

_____

7. (trust) _____

_____

8. (may) _____

_____

# V.  STORY COMPLETION

**Discuss or think about these questions before completing the story that follows.**

1. Why do we say that a dog is man's best friend?
2. We also say that a barking dog doesn't bite. Do you think that's true?
3. What does the sign "Beware of the Dog" mean?

**Complete the story with these words.**

| bites | afraid | a lot | however | may |
|---|---|---|---|---|
| a lot of | protects | own | trusts | |

### A Barking Dog

They say that a dog is man's best friend, and I believe that because I
_____ a dog and she's very friendly.  I love her
_____ .  Her name is Sandy.  She's intelligent and she can do
_____ things.

They also say that a barking dog doesn't bite.  You _____ believe
that, too, but I don't.  The dog who lives across the street from me barks at everyone,
and he also _____ .  No one _____ the dog.
_____ , the dog's owner is happy that everyone is
_____ of his dog.  He's rich, and the dog
_____ him and his house.  In front of his house he has a sign that
says, "Beware of the Dog."

# VI.  SHARING INFORMATION

**Discuss these questions and topics in pairs or small groups.**

1. Complete these sentences:  I eat **a lot of** _____ .  I _____
   **a lot.**

2. Are you **afraid** of dogs?  Mice?  Snakes?  Any other animals?  If so, which ones?

3. Complete this sentence:  I don't have a _____ , but I would like to
   **own** one.

4. Some people have dogs to **protect** themselves and their homes.  What other things do
   people use to protect themselves and their homes?

5. Complete the following sentence: There are many good things about living in the

   United States. **However,** _____

   _____ .

6. Some dogs **bite**. What other animals will bite people? What insect often bites?

7. In general, how much do you **trust** doctors, lawyers, teachers, police officers? Give them a number between one and ten. If you have complete trust, give them a ten. If you have no trust, give them a one.

8. Complete this sentence: Tomorrow I **may** _____ .

   I'm not sure.

# VII.  WORD FAMILIES

**Complete the sentences with these words.** *If necessary, add an ending to the word so it forms a correct sentence.* (adj. = adjective and adv. = adverb)

1. **own** (verb or adj.)              **owner** (noun)

   A. Where is the _____ of this car? It has to be moved.

   B. Ray is a pilot and _____ a small plane.

2. **protect** (verb)                 **protection** (noun)
   **protective** (adj.)              **protector** (noun)

   A. Parts of the city need more police _____ .

   B. When I was a little child, my older brother was my _____ .

   C. Put on these gloves. They'll _____ your hands.

   D. Some parents are too _____ of their children.

3. **trust** (verb or noun)            **trusting** (adj.)

   A. "In God we _____ " is printed on all U.S. coins and bills.

   B. Jenny believes everything she reads. She's too _____ .

20

# VIII. BUILDING NOUNS WITH -ER (-OR)

The suffix **-er** (sometimes **-or**) is added to many verbs to form a noun. For example, *teach + er = teacher; act + or = actor; wash + er = washer.*

When **-er** (or **-or**) is added to a verb, it means a person or thing that does something. For example, a *teacher* is *a person who teaches*; an *actor* is *a person who acts*; a *washer* is *a machine that washes.*

| Verb | Noun | Verb | Noun |
|------|------|------|------|
| act | actor | own | owner |
| dance | dancer | paint | painter |
| direct | director | play | player |
| drive | driver | sing | singer |
| dry | dryer | teach | teacher |
| freeze | freezer | work | worker |
| lead | leader | wash | washer |

**Add *-er*, *-or*, or *-r* to the following verbs, and use the nouns you form to complete the sentences.** *Add an s to the nouns if necessary.*

**dry**      **sing**      **write**      **freeze**      **teach**      **wash**

1. The history _____ is giving her class a test today.

2. I like O. Henry's short stories. He was a good _____.

3. Take the clothes out of the _____ and put them in the _____.

4. There's some ice cream in the _____.

5. Sylvia has a nice voice, but she's not a great _____.

**own**      **play**      **lead**      **act**      **drive**

6. Abraham Lincoln was a great _____.

7. Emily is taking us to the airport. I hope that she's a good _____.

8. Joe DiMaggio was a famous baseball _____.

9. The _____ are getting ready for the play.

10. I like that house, and I hear that the _____ wants to sell it.

# C H A P T E R  T H R E E
# *Fish for Dinner*

## PREVIEW QUESTIONS

**Discuss or think about these questions before reading the story.**

1. Do you want to lose weight, gain weight, or stay the same?
2. In the last year have you gained weight, lost weight, or stayed the same?
3. Many people in the United States go on diets to lose weight. Is this as common in other countries? If not, why not?

# Fish for Dinner

Tomiko is short and a little heavy. She's **only** five feet two inches tall, and she **weighs** 125 pounds. That's not bad; the problem is that she's gaining **weight**. When she came to Boston, she weighed only 110 pounds. She knows she'll feel and look better if she **loses** a little weight.

Three other people in Tomiko's office are also on a diet, but that's not surprising. In the United States, it seems that everyone is on a diet or thinking about one. Go to any bookstore, and you'll see many diet books, and all of them will show you a different way to lose weight.

Tomiko started her diet yesterday morning. "I want to lose ten pounds," she says, "but I'm not in a hurry. I know that most people who lose weight quickly gain it back. My friend, Rose, went on a diet and lost 15 pounds in a month. Three months later, she weighed more than when she started her diet."

**Although** Tomiko is **trying** to lose only a pound or two a week, it's hard. The problem is that she loves to eat. She especially loves ice cream and chocolate candy, but she can't have them on her diet.

Tomiko has been very good today. She had orange juice, cereal, and a cup of black coffee for breakfast. For lunch, she had a lettuce and tomato salad and some soup. She hasn't had anything between meals.

It's **almost** 6:00 now and Tomiko is **starving**. She's having fish, carrots, and broccoli for dinner. She **enjoys** fish, and vegetables are her favorite food. That's great because vegetables are good for you, and they don't have many calories.*

---

*A **calorie** tells *how much heat or energy a food has*. "An apple has about 80 **calories**."

# I. COMPREHENSION QUESTIONS

**Answer these questions about the story.** *Use your judgment to answer questions with an asterisk(*). Work in pairs or small groups. The numbers in parentheses show which paragraph in the story has the answer.*

1. How tall is Tomiko? (1)
2. How much does she weigh? (1)
*3. Why do you think she gained weight when she came to Boston?
4. What does it seem that everyone in the United States is doing or thinking about? (2)
5. How many pounds does Tomiko want to lose? (3)
6. Why isn't she in a hurry to lose weight? (3)

*7. Why is it bad to lose weight too quickly?

8. Why is it hard for Tomiko to lose weight? (4)

9. What does she especially love to eat? (4)

10. What did she have for breakfast? (5)

11. Why are vegetables great for her? (6)

*12. Do you think she will lose the ten pounds? Explain your answer.

# II.  WORD GUESSING

**Guess the meaning of the key words in these sentences.** *Use the context of the story and the sentences to guess. Circle your answers.*

1. Tomiko *is* **trying** *to lose* only a pound or two a week.

    a.  is not able to lose     c.  is doing what she can to lose

    b.  is thinking about losing     d.  doesn't want to lose

2. It's almost 6:00 and Tomiko is **starving**.

    a.  cooking     c.  resting

    b.  happy     d.  very hungry

3. Tomiko **enjoys** fish, and vegetables are her favorite food.

    a.  eats     c.  doesn't like

    b.  likes     d.  buys

# III.  MINI-DICTIONARY — PART ONE

## *Vocabulary Focus*

    1. **on·ly** (ōn′lē)   *adverb*:  and no more; and no other

                    *adjective*:  and nothing else; and no one else

    "We go to the beach **only** in the summer.  It's too cold in the spring, fall, and winter."

    "Paul was the **only** student who did well on the test.  All the others did poorly."

    2. A. **weight** (wāt)   *noun*:  how heavy a person or thing is

      "The baby is getting big.  What's his **weight**?"

      B. **weigh** (wā)     *verb*:  to have a weight of; to be a certain weight

      "The small bags of potatoes **weigh** five pounds."

24

3. **lose** (lōōz) *verb:* A. to have something and then not be able to find it

                     B. to have less of something

                     C. to fail to win; to be defeated

"I don't know where my ring is. I hope I didn't **lose** it."

"Gabe is **losing** his hair. He's not so young anymore."

"Our football team **lost** last Saturday. The other team was bigger and better."

The past tense of **lose** is **lost**.

4. **al·though** (ôl-thō´) *conjunction:* in contrast to the fact that*

"**Although** Tiffany studied hard for the test, she didn't pass."

*****Though** has the same meaning and is used in the same way as **although**.

"**Though** Tiffany studied hard for the test, she didn't pass."

## Completing Sentences

**Complete the sentences with these words.** *Use each word twice. Where a word has different endings, both forms are given.*

| losing/lost | only | weigh/weight | although |
|---|---|---|---|

1. The radio is ———————— $20. I'm going to buy it.

2. ———————— I slept well last night, I feel tired.

3. Leslie ———————— her keys and can't find them.

4. Roger looks thin. How much does he ————————?

5. Glen smokes a lot ———————— he knows he shouldn't.

6. Audrey has a ———————— problem. She's over 200 pounds.

7. The basketball is soft. It's ———————— air.

8. ———————— Donna knows where the money is.

## Creating Sentences

**Write an original sentence using these words.** *Work with a partner or on your own.*

1. (only) ————————————————————————————

2. (weigh) ————————————————————————————

3. (lose) ————————————————————————————

4. (although) ————————————————————————————

# IV. MINI-DICTIONARY — PART TWO

## Vocabulary Focus

5. **try** (trī)   *verb:* to do what one can; to make an effort
   *noun:* an effort
   "Carlos is **trying** to learn English quickly."
   "Joan didn't catch the ball, but she made a nice **try**."

6. **al·most** (ôl´mōst *or* ôl-mōst´)   *adverb:* a little less than; be close to
   "It's **almost** a mile to the supermarket."

7. **starve** (stärv)   *verb:* A. to be very hungry  B. to die because one has no food
   "Sandra didn't eat breakfast.  She must be **starving**."
   "In the winter, some animals **starve** because they can't find food."

8. **en·joy** (in-joi´)   *verb:* to like; to get pleasure from
   "Dick **enjoys** playing cards with his friends."

## Completing Sentences

**Complete the sentences with these words.**  *Use each word twice.  Where a word has different endings, both forms are given.*

enjoy/enjoyed          try/trying          almost          starve/starving

1. Let's eat now.  I'm _____ .

2. Brenda is _____ to find a better job.  She wants to make more money.

3. I _____ cut myself with that knife.

4. We _____ the movie.  It was interesting.

5. Are the children _____ ready to go to school?

6. We always feed the birds when it snows.  We don't want them to

   _____ .

7. _____ yourself at the party!

8. I may not be able to climb to the top of the mountain, but I'm going to

   _____ .

## *Creating Sentences*

**Write an original sentence using these words.** *Work with a partner or on your own.*

5. (try) _____

6. (almost) _____

7. (starve) _____

8. (enjoy) _____

# V.  STORY COMPLETION

**Discuss or think about these questions before completing the story that follows.**

1. Name some foods that have a lot of calories.
2. Name some low in calories.
3. Why are some people thin although they eat a lot?

### Complete the story with these words.

| lose | almost | trying | weight | starving |
|---|---|---|---|---|
| although | only | weighs | enjoys | |

### *Very Different Problems*

My friend Rafael _____ 105 pounds _____ he eats a lot and _____ big meals. He's _____ to gain 15 pounds, but up to now he's been able to gain _____ one.

I have a very different problem. I'm 220 pounds and want to _____ 30. That's why I'm on a diet, but so far my _____ hasn't changed.

It's _____ time for lunch, and Rafael and I are _____. We're going to a diner. I'm having a small tuna fish salad and a diet Coke. He's getting a large cheeseburger, french fries, and apple pie with vanilla ice cream.

27

# VI.  SHARING INFORMATION

**Discuss these questions and topics in pairs or small groups.**

1. When a family has **only** one child, we say that boy or girl is an only child.  Are you an only child?  If not, how many brothers do you have?  And sisters?

2. Some people go on a diet, lose a lot of **weight**, and then gain it all back.  Do you know anyone who did this?  Did you ever do it?

3. Did you ever **lose** anything that was valuable, for example, a ring, watch, money, or important papers?  If so, how did it happen?  Did you find it (or them) again?

4. Complete this sentence:  **Although** I don't like to _____

   _____, I have to.

5. Think about what you do, and complete this sentence:  I'm **trying** to _____

   _____.

6. Tell about something that **almost** happened to you, for example, an accident.  Or tell about something you almost did.

7. **Starve** usually means *to be very hungry*, but it also means *to die because there is nothing to eat*.  Is there any part of the world where people still starve?  If so, where?  Why is there little or no food there?

8. Name some activities that you **enjoy**.

# VII.  WORD FAMILIES

**Complete the sentences with these words.**  *If necessary, add an ending to the word so it forms a correct sentence.*  (adj. = adjective and adv. = adverb)

1. **lose** (verb)　　　　**loser** (noun)　　　　**loss** (noun)　　　　**lost** (adj.)

   A. When I play tennis, I try hard to win, but I also know how to be a good

      _____ .

   B. Jessica is upset about the _____ of her watch.

   C. As soon as I get my paycheck, I put it in my wallet. I don't want to

      _____ it.

   D. We're looking for a _____ dog.  I hope we find him soon.

28

2. **starve** (verb)                      **starvation** (noun)

    A. In the winter of 1620–1621, the Pilgrims who came to Plymouth, Massachusetts,

       faced _____ .

    B. When my son comes home from school, he goes to the kitchen to get something

       to eat. He's _____ .

3. **enjoy** (verb)            **enjoyment** (noun)            **enjoyable** (adj.)

    A. Linda gets a lot of _____ from playing the piano.

    B. I hope you _____ the play.

    C. Our trip to Florida was _____ .

# VIII. BUILDING NOUNS WITH -MENT

The suffix **-ment** is added to verbs to form a noun. For example, *pay + ment = payment; command + ment = commandment.*

When **-ment** is added to a verb, it usually means *the act of* or *the result of.* For example, *a payment* is *the act or result of paying; a commandment* is *the result of giving a command.*

| Verb | Noun | Verb | Noun |
| --- | --- | --- | --- |
| advance | advancement | govern | government |
| announce | announcement | judge | judgment |
| appoint | appointment | move | movement |
| arrange | arrangement | pay | payment |
| command | commandment | place | placement |
| employ | employment | state | statement |
| enjoy | enjoyment | | |

**Circle the letter next to the word that *best* completes the sentence.**

1. I have one more _____ to make on my new car.
   - a. statement
   - b. movement
   - c. payment
   - d. placement

2. The _____ for our trip to Hawaii are complete.
   - a. advancements
   - b. arrangements
   - c. announcements
   - d. judgments

3. Riding her new bicycle is giving Gina a lot of _____.
   - a. employment
   - b. advancement
   - c. movement
   - d. enjoyment

4. The president is going to make some important _____ on TV tonight.
   - a. announcements
   - b. placements
   - c. arrangements
   - d. judgments

5. You made a _____ about me that I don't like.
   - a. commandment
   - b. appointment
   - c. movement
   - d. statement

6. The United States and France have strong central _____.
   - a. arrangements
   - b. placements
   - c. governments
   - d. employment

7. People are living longer today because of _____ in the field of medicine.
   - a. appointments
   - b. advancements
   - c. statements
   - d. judgments

8. The exam helps in the _____ of the students in the right classes.
   - a. placement
   - b. announcement
   - c. employment
   - d. payment

# IX.  MAP READING

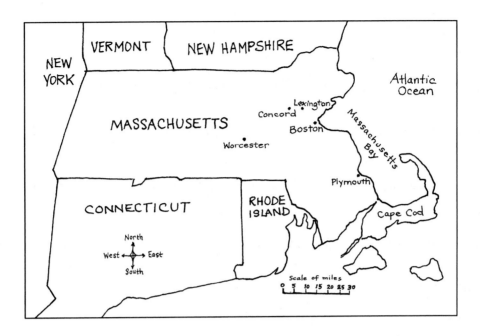

## *Massachusetts*

**Answer these questions about Massachusetts, Tomiko's new home.**

1. What two states are south of Massachusetts?
2. What two states are north of Massachusetts?
3. What state is west of Massachusetts?
4. Are Lexington and Concord northeast or northwest of Boston?
5. Is Plymouth southeast or southwest of Boston?
6. What famous cape is southeast of Boston?
7. On what ocean is the coast of Massachusetts?
8. About how many miles is it from Boston to Worcester?

## *Homework*

Bring to class a map of the state in which you live.  Work with a partner and make up ten questions about your state.

# UNIT ONE WORD REVIEW

## I.  SYNONYMS

Next to each sentence, write the word that has the same meaning or almost the same meaning as the part of the sentence in dark print.

| | | | |
|---|---|---|---|
| starving | hurries | a lot of | missed |
| have to | almost | only | enjoys |

1. _____ The southern part of the United States doesn't get **much** snow.

2. _____ It's been a long trip, but we're **close to** home now.

3. _____ Ron **wasn't at** the meeting.  He didn't feel well.

4. _____ Hillary **likes** her science and history classes.

5. _____ I have a friend who never **moves fast**.

6. _____ **No one but** Sam has a key to the office.

7. _____ We **must** finish the job today.

8. _____ Is there a restaurant near here?  I'm **very hungry**.

## II.  SENTENCE COMPLETION

Complete the sentences with these words.

| | | | |
|---|---|---|---|
| quickly | far | may | however |
| trying | owns | around | waste |

1. I'm going to have my eyes examined.  I _____ need glasses.

2. Barbara _____ a motor boat that she uses a lot in the summer.

3. Many people _____ water because it's cheap.

4. Felix is _____ to do better in school.

5. Drew and Terry did the dishes _____ and went to an early movie.

32

6. A new electronic typewriter costs _____ $150.

7. Is it _____ from here to your parents' house?

8. Norma is 85; _____, she's very active.

# III. STORY COMPLETION

**Complete the story with these words.**

afraid                  lose                  weighs                  trust

protect                 bite                  too                     although

*Lions*

Lions are the largest members of the cat family.   An adult lion _____ 400 pounds. _____ the lion is the king of the animal world, it spends most of the day sleeping and resting.

Lions live in groups, and they attack, _____ , and kill other animals.  For this reason, no animals _____ them.

India and some countries in Africa have laws to _____ lions because people have killed _____ many of them.  These countries are _____ that without these laws, they will _____ all of their lions.

33

# UNIT TWO

# A Young Couple

# CHAPTER FOUR
# *Sharing the Housework*

## PREVIEW QUESTIONS

**Discuss or think about these questions before reading the story.**

1. Why is it difficult to be a taxi driver in a large city like New York?
2. Why is it also good to be a taxi driver in a large city?
3. When a wife works full time, do most husbands do half of the housework?  If not, why not?

# Sharing the Housework

Frank and Sue are married and have two young children. Frank is a taxi driver in New York City, one of the best cities in the world to be a taxi driver in, and also one of the worst.[1] It's one of the best because you never have to wait long for passengers, and taxis cost a lot, so you can make good money. It's one of the worst because traffic is heavy, and everyone is in a hurry.

When Frank and Sue got married, they thought she would stay home and take care of the children, and he would make the money to pay the bills. But that's not the way it is. Food, clothing, and their new house cost more than he makes. Sue has to work, too. She's a teacher's aide at P.S. 63 in Manhattan.[2]

Since **both** of them work, Frank and Sue **share** the housework. "That's the way it should be," Sue says, "but some of my friends work full time and their husbands don't do any housework. Frank does all of the cooking, and I keep the house clean and wash the clothes."

Frank had never cooked in his life. The first night he tried, he **burned** the rice, and the chicken didn't taste right. Frank and Sue **still** laugh about his first dinner. He'll never be a great cook, but he's **improving** fast. He likes to cook spaghetti and meatballs, and they taste very good. Learning to cook was difficult for Frank, but now he thinks it's **fun**.

When Frank cooks, Sue washes the dishes and he **wipes** them. Although he likes to cook, he **hates** to do dishes. That's why he wants to buy a dishwasher. Sue also thinks it's a good idea, but they don't have any extra money now.

When they finish the dishes and the children are in bed, Frank and Sue read, watch TV, or talk. It's the only time during the day when they have the chance to enjoy a little peace and quiet. Their work and their children don't leave them much time for themselves.

---

[1] **Best** is the superlative of **good**; **better** is the comparative. **Worst** is the superlative of **bad**; **worse** is the comparative.
[2] **P.S.** = public school. **Manhattan** is one of the five boroughs, or divisions, of New York City.


# I.   COMPREHENSION QUESTIONS

**Answer these questions about the story.** *Use your judgment to answer questions with an asterisk(\*). Work in pairs or small groups. The numbers in parentheses show which paragraph in the story has the answer.*

1. Why is New York City one of the best places to be a taxi driver? (1)

2. Why is it one of the worst? (1)

*3. Compare driving a cab in a small city to driving one in New York? What are some of the differences?

4. Why does Sue have to work? (2)

*5. What do teachers' aides do? How do they help teachers?

6. What happens to some of Sue's friends? (3)

*7. Do you think these friends are angry with their husbands because they don't help with the housework? Explain your answer.

8. What happened the first night Frank cooked? (4)

9. What does he like to cook? (4)

10. What does he hate to do? (5)

11. What do Frank and Sue want to buy? Why can't they? (5)

12. When do they enjoy a little peace and quiet? (6)

# II. WORD GUESSING

**Guess the meaning of the key words in these sentences.** *Use the context of the story and the sentences to guess. Circle your answers.*

1. Since both of them work, Frank and Sue **share** the housework.

    a. don't do             c. pay someone to do

    b. do...later           d. divide

2. Frank will never be a great cook, but he's **improving** fast.

    a. getting better        c. working

    b. changing            d. getting worse

3. Although Frank likes to cook, he **hates** *to* do dishes.

    a. also likes to        c. also has to

    b. doesn't like to     d. won't

# III. MINI-DICTIONARY — PART ONE

## *Vocabulary Focus*

1. **both** (bōth) *adjective and pronoun:* the one and the other; the two
    "**Both** dresses are pretty, but I can buy only one."
    "Ramón and Alice are friends, and **both** are lawyers."

2. **share** (shâr)    *verb:* to do or use with others; to divide

                *noun:* the part of something one owns, does, or uses with others

     "Roberta bought a box of candy and **shared** it with her friends."

     "George is lazy; he doesn't do his **share** of the work."

3. **burn** (bûrn)    *verb:* A. to be on fire; to destroy by heat

                   B. to hurt by fire or heat

               *noun:* injury caused by fire or heat

     "The building is **burning**! Call the fire department!"

     "The plate is hot. If you touch it, you'll **burn** your fingers."

     "Esther was in a fire. She has **burns** on her face and arms."

4. **still** (stil)    *adverb:* A. up to now and at this time, too*

                    B. up to then and at that time, too

     "It's 11:00 P.M. and Greg is **still** studying."

     "When I left the office, the boss was **still** working."

     *****Still** can also mean *not moving.* "Be **still**. Stop kicking the chair."

## Completing Sentences

**Complete the sentences with these words.** *Use each word twice. Where a word has different endings, both forms are given.*

| burn/burning | still | share/shares | both |
|---|---|---|---|

1. I'm pleased when my older son _____ his toys with his brother.

2. Our basketball team won by 15 points, but _____ teams played well.

3. Is it _____ snowing?

4. Be careful with that hot iron! Don't _____ yourself!

5. Miss Martinez is a better teacher than Mrs. Allan, but _____ are

    very good.

6. Does your daughter _____ want to be a dentist?

7. If we win the lottery, we'll _____ the money.

8. I smell smoke. What's _____ ?

39

## Creating Sentences

**Write an original sentence using these words.** *Work with a partner or on your own.*

1. (both) _____

   _____

2. (share) _____

   _____

3. (burn) _____

   _____

4. (still) _____

   _____


# IV.  MINI-DICTIONARY — PART TWO

## Vocabulary Focus

5. **im·prove** (im-prŌŌv´)  *verb:* to do or become better
   "Chen still makes a lot of errors, but his English is **improving**."

6. **fun** (fun)  *noun:* pleasure; a good time
   "I love to dance. It's **fun**."

7. **wipe** (wῑp)  *verb:* to move a cloth over something to clean or dry it
   "The waiter cleared and **wiped** the table."

8. **hate** (hāt)  *verb:* to dislike strongly
   *noun:* strong dislike
   "Our son **hates** to clean his room."
   "**Hate** is the opposite of love."

## Completing Sentences

**Complete the sentences with these words.** *Use each word twice. Where a word has different endings, both forms are given.*

wipe/wiping          hate/hates          fun          improves/improving

1. Have _____ at the picnic!

2. Cathy is _____ the baby's hands and face.

3. I hope the weather _____ . It's not very good, and we want to play

   golf this afternoon.

4. Bob loves to talk on the phone, but he _____ to write letters.

5. _____ your shoes on the mat before you go into the house. They're dirty.

6. We spent three days at Disney World, and we had a lot of _____ .

7. I _____ to be late for work.

8. Pat doesn't play the guitar very well, but she's taking lessons and she's _____ .

## Creating Sentences

**Write an original sentence using these words.** *Work with a partner or on your own.*

5. (improve) _____

   _____

6. (fun) _____

   _____

7. (wipe) _____

   _____

8. (hate) _____

   _____

# V. STORY COMPLETION

**Discuss or think about these questions before completing the story that follows.**

1. Do you spend much time in the sun in the summer?

2. Why is it bad to get too much sun?

3. What can we do to protect our skin from the sun?

**Complete the story with these words.**

| | | | |
|---|---|---|---|
| wiped | still | improving | share |
| hates | both | fun | burn |

### Too Much Sun

Sharon and Helen graduated from college last year. _____ of them work for International Business Machines (IBM). Sharon sells computers, and Helen is a computer programmer. They're single and they _____ an apartment.

Sharon and Helen like to swim, and yesterday was a warm, sunny day. So they went to the beach and had a lot of _____. After Sharon went for a swim, she _____ her face and arms with a towel and lay in the sun. She wished she hadn't. She got a very bad _____, and it _____ hurts today.

Helen thinks Sharon should see a doctor, but she _____ to go to doctors. She says she's _____ and will be fine in a few days. She thinks going to a doctor would be a waste of time and money.

# VI.  SHARING INFORMATION

**Discuss these questions and topics in pairs or small groups.**

1. Complete the following sentence about the United States and Canada: **Both** countries

   _____.

2. Give an example of something you **share** or **shared** with others. Why is sharing so important?

3. Did you ever **burn** yourself? How? Was the burn bad? Did you put anything on it? Did you have to see a doctor?

4. What city did you live in last year? Do you **still** live in the same city?

5. Why are you studying English? Is your English **improving**? What are you doing to improve it?

6. Name some things that are **fun** to do.

7. All cars, buses, and trucks have **wipers**. Where are the wipers, and what do they do?

8. Name some things that you **hate** to do.

# VII. WORD FAMILIES

**Complete the sentences with these words.** *If necessary, add an ending to the word so it forms a correct sentence.* (adj. = adjective and adv. = adverb)

1. **burn** (verb or noun)       **burner** (noun)

    A. We have a new oil _____. It's much better than our old one.

    B. Is the fire still _____?

2. **improve** (verb)       **improvement** (noun)

    A. Your school work was poor last year. I want to see some

    _____ this year.

    B. Sal had a heart attack, but he's _____ and will leave the hospital

    soon.

3. **fun** (noun)       **funny*** (adj.)

    A. Marge and I go bowling every Friday night. It's _____.

    B. Everyone laughed at the clown. He was very _____.

    >*Fun** and **funny** have different meanings. **Fun** means *a good time*. **Funny** means *causing laughter or a smile*.

4. **hate** (verb or noun)       **hatred** (noun)

    A. Rosa is from the Dominican Republic, and she _____ cold weather.

    *B. _____ can easily lead to fighting and violence.

    *There are two possible answers to B.

43

# VIII. BUILDING ADJECTIVES WITH -Y

The suffix **-y** is added to nouns to form an adjective, for example, *dirt + y = dirty*; *rain + y = rainy*.

When **-y** is added to a noun to form an adjective, it usually means *full of* or *a lot of*. For example, *dirty* means *full of* or *a lot of dirt*; *rainy* means *a lot of rain*.

| Noun | Adjective | Noun | Adjective |
|------|-----------|------|-----------|
| dirt | dirty | rain | rainy |
| fun | funny | rock | rocky |
| health | healthy | salt | salty |
| ice | icy | sun | sunny |
| juice | juicy | thirst | thirsty |
| luck | lucky | wind | windy |
| noise | noisy | | |

**Circle the letter next to the word that *best* completes the sentence.**

1. I want a soda; I'm _____ .

      a. healthy        c. thirsty

      b. lucky        d. dirty

2. There are no clouds in the sky. It's going to be a _____ day.

      a. windy        c. healthy

      b. noisy        d. sunny

3. Our team was _____ . That's why we won the game.

      a. thirsty        c. funny

      b. lucky        d. rocky

4. These clothes are _____ . I have to wash them.

      a. dirty        c. juicy

      b. salty        d. rocky

5. A lot of people were at the party. It was _____ .

      a. lucky        c. healthy

      b. noisy        d. windy

6. These oranges are _____ .
        a. icy           c. dirty
        b. salty        d. juicy

7. Be careful! The streets and sidewalks are _____ .
        a. rocky       c. icy
        b. windy      d. rainy

8. I don't like the way this food tastes. It's too _____ .
        a. salty       c. dirty
        b. healthy    d. juicy

# CHAPTER FIVE

# *Rushing the Baby to the Hospital*

## ? ? ? ? ? ? ? ? ? ? ? ? ? ? ? ? ? ? ? ? ? ? ? ? ?
## PREVIEW QUESTIONS

**Discuss or think about these questions before reading the story.**

1. Why is the first grade so important in a child's education?
2. Babies love to touch things.  Why is this good?
3. What things do we have to keep away from babies?

# Rushing the Baby to the Hospital

Frank and Sue have a son and daughter, and they're very **proud** of them. Their son's name is Frank, and they call him Frankie. He's six years old and in the first grade. He's a good student and he enjoys school. He's learning to read and add.

After school, Frankie plays with his friends. "Baseball is my favorite sport," he says, "and I love to play catch with my dad. In the summer he takes me to some Yankee games.[1] I'm going to play for the Yankees some day."

Their daughter is two years old, and her name is Sarah. She's beginning to talk. She's a very active baby who likes to **explore** and touch everything. Now that's great because that's the way a baby learns, but it's also a problem. You have to watch Sarah all the time. **Fortunately**, Sue's mom lives near Sue and Frank, and she takes care of the baby when Sue is working. Grandma loves this; she thinks Sarah is the cutest baby in the world.

Frank and Sue are careful not to put medicine or cleaning materials where Sarah can get them. They keep their medicine in the bathroom cabinet. They're afraid Sarah might think it's candy and take some. And they keep cleaning materials in a cabinet over the kitchen sink.

However, last Saturday Sue left a bottle of bleach[2] under the kitchen sink. That was a big **mistake**. Sarah was playing in the kitchen, and she **swallowed** some bleach. Bleach is a **poison** that can kill a baby. Fortunately, Sue saw what happened.

Frank and Sue didn't waste a second. They **rushed** Sarah to the hospital. It's about a mile from their house. They got there in two minutes. The doctor talked to Sue because he had to know what the baby swallowed.

The doctor examined Sarah and gave her some medicine. They kept her in the hospital for five hours and watched her. Fortunately, she swallowed only a little **bit** of bleach and was okay. When she arrived home, she got a lot of hugs and kisses from her grandmother and Frankie.

---

[1] The New York Yankees are a major league baseball team. They play in the Bronx, which is part of New York City.
[2] **Bleach** is *a liquid or powder used to make clothes brighter.*

# I. COMPREHENSION QUESTIONS

## *True or False*

**If the sentence is true, write *T*.  If it's false, write *F* and change it to a true statement.**

_____ 1. Frankie doesn't like school.

_____

_____ 2. Baseball is his favorite sport.

_____

_____ 3. It's easy to take care of Sarah.

_____

_____ 4. Frank and Sue keep their medicine in the bathroom cabinet.

_____

_____ 5. Sue left some bleach where Sarah could get it.

_____

_____ 6. Frank and Sue got to the hospital quickly.

_____

_____ 7. Sarah spent two days in the hospital.

_____

_____ 8. She swallowed a lot of bleach.

_____

## What Do You Think?

**Use your experience, judgment, and the story to answer these questions.** *The story alone won't answer them.*

1. Frank plays with his son and takes him to baseball games. Is that important? If so, why?

2. Frankie thinks he's going to play for the Yankees. Do you think his parents should let him think that? Or should they tell him it'll probably never happen? Explain your answer.

3. Grandparents are almost always easier on children than parents. For example, they correct them less. Why?

4. Do you think Frank got angry at Sue for leaving the bleach under the sink? Do you think he said anything to her? Explain your answer.

# II.  WORD GUESSING

**Guess the meaning of the key words in these sentences.** *Use the context of the story and the sentences to guess. Circle your answers.*

1. Sarah is a very active baby who likes to **explore** and touch everything.
   - a. play
   - b. look at things carefully
   - c. laugh
   - d. cry

2. Sue left a bottle of bleach under the kitchen sink. That was a big **mistake**.
   - a. fear
   - b. loss
   - c. error
   - d. improvement

3. Sarah was playing in the kitchen and **swallowed** some bleach.
   - a. touched
   - b. opened
   - c. smelled
   - d. drank

# III.  MINI-DICTIONARY — PART ONE

## Vocabulary Focus

1. **proud** (of) (proud)     *adjective:*  A.  very happy with what one has or does

     B.  having too high opinion of oneself

   "Joe is **proud** of his wife. She's smart and very nice."

   "Dennis thinks he's better than anyone else. He's **proud**."

2. **ex·plore** (ək-splôr´)  *verb:*  A.  to go through and look carefully at an area

   B.  to look carefully at an idea or thing

   "Columbus **explored** the Caribbean and many of its islands."

   "Doctors are **exploring** new ways of treating cancer."

3. **for·tu·nate·ly** (fôr´chə-nit-lē)   *adverb:*  by good luck; luckily

   "Ling lost the key to her car.  **Fortunately**, she had another one."

4. **mis·take** (mi-stāk´)   *noun:*  error

   *verb:*  to think that one thing or person is another

   "No one is perfect.  We all make **mistakes**."

   "I frequently **mistake** Tom for his twin brother."

## *Completing Sentences*

**Complete the sentences with these words.** *Use each word twice. Where a word has different endings, both forms are given.*

| fortunately | explore/explored | proud | mistake/mistakes |
|---|---|---|---|

1. I don't like this book.  It was a _____ to buy it.

2. Exxon _____ the area for oil, but didn't find any.

3. Kristin is _____ of her new car.

4. We went to the park for a picnic.  _____, the weather was nice.

5. Psychiatrists _____ people's feelings and lives.

6. I got an A in math.  I'm _____ of myself.

7. Leo was in an auto accident.  _____, he was wearing a seat belt and

   wasn't hurt.

8. Laura wrote an interesting composition, but she made a lot of spelling

   _____ .

## Creating Sentences

**Write an original sentence using these words.** *Work with a partner or on your own.*

1. (proud) _____

2. (explore) _____

3. (fortunately) _____

4. (mistake) _____

# IV.  MINI-DICTIONARY — PART TWO

## Vocabulary Focus

5. **swal·low** (swol´ō)    *verb:* to move food or drink down the throat
   *noun:* the act of swallowing; the amount swallowed
   "These pills are large.  It's difficult to **swallow** them."
   "I'm thirsty.  Let me have a **swallow** of your soda, please."

6. **poi·son** (poi´zən)    *noun:* a substance that can kill
   *verb:* to kill or hurt with poison
   "Someone put **poison** in the cat's food and killed her."
   "The smoke from the factories is **poisoning** our air."

7. **rush** (rush)    *verb:* to move fast; to hurry
   *noun:* the act of moving fast
   "The fire engines are **rushing** to the fire."
   "Abdul can't wait for us.  He's in a **rush**."

8. **bit** (bit)    *noun:* a small amount
   "We need some fresh air in this room.  Please open the window a **bit**."

## Completing Sentences

**Complete the sentences with these words.** *Use each word twice. Where a word has different endings, both forms are given.*

poison/poisoning          rush/rushes          bit          swallow/swallowing

1. Mike is lazy. He didn't do a _____ of work today.

2. Debbie _____ home from work every afternoon.

3. I have a sore throat. It hurts to _____.

4. The soldiers were afraid that the enemy would use _____ gas.

5. Chew your food well before _____ it.

6. The ice cream tastes very good. May I have a _____ more?

7. The chemicals we're using to kill insects are _____ our water.

8. What's your _____? We're not going anywhere.

## Creating Sentences

**Write an original sentence using these words.** *Work with a partner or on your own.*

5. (swallow) _____

_____

6. (poison) _____

_____

7. (rush) _____

_____

8. (bit) _____

_____

# V.  STORY COMPLETION

**Discuss or think about these questions before completing the story that follows.**

1. Why is it easier to care for a dog in the country than in a city?
2. Are you afraid of mice?  If so, why?
3. What do people use to kill mice?

### Complete the story with these words.

| | | | |
|---|---|---|---|
| mistake | rushed | proud | fortunately |
| bit | poison | swallowed | explore |

### *Vet\* Saves Dog*

Paul has a beautiful dog named Wolf and a nice house in the country.  Paul and Wolf like to go for long walks and to _____ the woods near his house.  Paul is _____ of his dog and house, but there's a problem with the house.  When the weather turns cold, mice from the fields get into it.  Paul isn't afraid of mice, but he doesn't like to have them running around his house.

Yesterday he bought some powder to _____ the mice.  He put the powder in a dish next to the refrigerator, and that was a _____ .  Wolf thought the powder was food, and he _____ some.  _____ , Paul had put only a _____ of powder in the dish.

When Wolf got sick, Paul knew it was the powder, and he _____ the dog to a veterinarian.\*  The vet was able to save Wolf.  On the way home, Paul bought some mousetraps and cheese.

\*A **veterinarian** is *an animal doctor* and is often called a **vet**.

53

# VI.  SHARING INFORMATION

**Discuss these questions and topics in pairs or small groups.**

1.  Complete the following sentence:  I'm **proud** of _____

    _____ .

2.  What are some of the good things that have come from the **exploration** of space by the United States and the former Soviet Union?

3.  Complete the following sentence:  I'm **fortunate** that _____

    _____ .

4.  Everyone makes **mistakes**.  Tell about a mistake that you or another person made.

5.  It's difficult to **swallow** food when your throat hurts.  What do people usually eat when they have a sore throat?

6.  Bleach is a **poison**.  Name some other **poisonous** things that are often in a home.

7.  Eight o'clock in the morning and 5:00 at night are called "**rush** hours."  Why?

8.  Sometimes we use "a **bit**" followed by an adjective, for example, "I'm a bit thirsty." Which of these sentences describe how you feel now?

    a.  I'm not tired.      a.  I'm not hungry.

    b.  I'm a *bit* tired.      b.  I'm a *bit* hungry.

    c.  I'm very tired.      c.  I'm very hungry.

# VII.  WORD FAMILIES

**Complete the sentences with these words.**  *If necessary, add an ending to the word so it forms a correct sentence.*  (adj. = adjective and adv. = adverb)

1.  **proud** (adj.)          **proudly** (adv.)          **pride** (noun)

    A.  Gladys is in the army and wears her uniform _____ .

    B.  Andy and Yuri are excellent carpenters.  They take _____ in

        their work.

    C.  We are _____ of our school.  It's one of the best in the state.

2. **explore** (verb)         **explorer** (noun)         **exploration** (noun)

A.  In the sixteenth century, Spain sent many _____ to North and South America.

B.  England and France were the leaders in the _____ of North America.

C.  Thomas Jefferson, the third president of the United States, sent Lewis and Clark to _____ the Louisiana Territory, which the United States had purchased from France.

3. **fortunately** (adv.)         **fortune** (noun)         **fortunate** (adj.)
   **unfortunate** (adj.)         **unfortunately** (adv.)

A.  I went to a casino in Atlantic City to try my luck. _____ , I lost a lot of money.

B.  Elena never gets sick. She's _____ .

C.  Someone stole my car. _____ , the police found it, and I got it back.

D.  It's _____ that the factory is closing. Many people will lose their jobs.

E.  No one knows what _____ will bring.

4. **mistake** (noun or verb)         **mistaken** (adj.)

A.  Many people come to the United States with the _____ idea that it's easy to get rich here.

B.  I put salt in the sugar bowl by _____ .

5. **poison** (noun or verb)         **poisonous** (adj.)

A.  The leaves of some plants contain _____ .

B.  Some snakes are _____ .

# VIII.   BUILDING WORDS WITH UN-

The prefix **un-** is placed before many adjectives, adverbs, and verbs to form a new word.

When **un-** is placed before an adjective or adverb, it means *not* or *the opposite of*, for example, *un + happy = unhappy*, which means *not happy*; *un + fortunately = unfortunately*, which means *the opposite of fortunately*.

When **un-** is placed before a verb, it indicates an action that is the opposite of that verb. For example, *un + dress = undress*; *un + lock = unlock*; *un + cover = uncover*; *un + do = undo*. *Undress, unlock, uncover*, and *undo* are the opposites of *dress, lock, cover*, and *do*.

| Adjective, Adverb, or Verb | New Word |
|---|---|
| able | unable |
| afraid | unafraid |
| cover | uncover |
| do | undo |
| dress | undress |
| fortunate | unfortunate |
| fortunately | unfortunately |
| happy | unhappy |
| healthy | unhealthy |
| important | unimportant |
| kind | unkind |
| lock | unlock |
| married | unmarried |
| necessary | unnecessary |
| safe | unsafe |
| true | untrue |

**Circle the letter next to the word that *best* completes the sentence.**

1. The meeting was ———————, but we had to go to it.
   - a. unkind
   - b. unimportant
   - c. unhealthy
   - d. untrue

2. The bridge is ———————. They have to fix it.
   - a. unnecessary
   - b. unhealthy
   - c. unfortunate
   - d. unsafe

3. Jean was ——————— to get the book she wanted.
   - a. unable
   - b. unafraid
   - c. unhappy
   - d. untrue

4. I don't like Amy. Sometimes she's ———————.
   - a. unfortunate
   - b. unnecessary
   - c. unkind
   - d. unsafe

5. Sid got ——————— and went to bed.
   - a. unlocked
   - b. undressed
   - c. unhappy
   - d. unafraid

6. My visit to the doctor was ———————. There was nothing wrong with me.
   - a. unnecessary
   - b. unsafe
   - c. unhealthy
   - d. unkind

7. Jeff is 30, rich, and handsome; and he's still ———————.
   - a. untrue
   - b. unfortunate
   - c. unafraid
   - d. unmarried

8. I hope you don't believe what Sally said about me. It was ———————.
   - a. unimportant
   - b. unkind
   - c. untrue
   - d. unnecessary

# CHAPTER SIX
# *Chevrolets, Fords, and Hondas*

## ? ? ? ? ? ? ? ? ? ? ? ? ? ? ? ? ? ? ? ? ? ? ? ?
## PREVIEW QUESTIONS

**Discuss or think about these questions before reading the story.**

1.  What are the problems with buying a used car?  Why do people buy them?

2.  How much does a new compact car — for example, a Honda Accord or Ford Taurus — cost?

3.  Do all car dealers charge the same price for the same car, or is it possible to get a lower price by shopping around?

# Chevrolets, Fords, and Hondas

Frank and Sue are going to buy a new car. Their car is 11 years old, and they're having a lot of problems with it; it also needs new tires. **Of course** they could have it fixed and buy new tires, but that would be **expensive** and a waste of money. They're trying to sell their old car for $250.

They thought about buying a used car to save money, but they decided not to. "If you buy a used car," says Frank, "you're buying another person's problems. We don't want to do that. We want a car that runs well and that we can trust." Naturally a new car will cost a lot, but Frank and Sue are hoping to find one that's not too expensive.

Frank and Sue's **neighbor**, Mr. Wallace, bought a new Cadillac last month. He's a good friend, and he let Frank drive his car. It's beautiful and it's big. Mr. Wallace loves it and Frank does, too, but it was very expensive. Mr. Wallace is a lawyer. He can **afford** a Cadillac, but Frank and Sue can't.

They're looking at Chevrolets, Fords, and Hondas. They're going from dealer to dealer, looking carefully and comparing prices. This takes a lot of time, but they plan to keep their new car for ten years. They know it would be a mistake to **choose** too quickly.

Yesterday they looked at a Honda Accord, and it's **just** what they want. It's not cheap, but it looks nice and it doesn't use a lot of gas. Everyone says that it's a great car. Frank took it for a test drive and he liked it. They plan to buy it.

They're going to the bank today to get a **loan**. It should be easy to get one since both of them are working, and they have always paid their bills on time. They have saved some money to buy a car, but they also have to **borrow** $5,000.

## I. COMPREHENSION QUESTIONS

**Answer these questions about the story.** *Use your judgment to answer questions with an asterisk(\*). Work in pairs or small groups. The numbers in parentheses show which paragraph in the story has the answer.*

1. Why are Frank and Sue buying a new car? (1)
2. Why don't they fix the car they have? (1)
*3. Why do you think it would be a waste of money to fix their car?
4. What does Frank say is the problem with buying a used car? (2)
*5. Do you agree with him? Explain your answer.
6. How do Frank and Mr. Wallace feel about his Cadillac? (3)
7. Why can Mr. Wallace afford a Cadillac? (3)
8. Why are Frank and Sue going from dealer to dealer? (4)

9. How long do they plan to keep their new car? (4)

10. Why are they going to buy a Honda Accord? (5)

*11. The Honda Accord is a Japanese car. Do you think that Japanese cars are generally better than American ones? Explain your answer.

12. Why should it be easy for Frank and Sue to get a car loan? Give two reasons. (6)

# II.  WORD GUESSING

**Guess the meaning of the key words in these sentences.** *Use the context of the story and the sentences to guess. Circle your answers.*

1. They could have the car fixed and buy new tires, but that would *be* **expensive**.

    a. be stupid          c. cost a lot

    b. be the best       d. be smart

2. Mr. Wallace is a lawyer. He can **afford** a Cadillac, but Frank and Sue can't.

    a. rent              c. fix

    b. pay for          d. think about

3. They know it would be a mistake to **choose** too quickly.

    a. go to the bank      c. make a decision

    b. drive             d. ask about the price

# III.  MINI-DICTIONARY — PART ONE

### *Vocabulary Focus*

1. **of course** (əv kôrs *or* ə-kôrs´)     *idiom:* naturally; certainly; clearly
    "**Of course** I love my children. Almost all parents do."

2. **ex·pen·sive** (ek-spen´siv)     *adjective:* costing a lot
    "Hilton hotels are very nice and very **expensive**."

3. **neigh·bor** (nā´bər)     *noun:* a person who lives near another
    "Juanita lives across the street from me. We're neighbors."

4. **af·ford** (ə-fôrd´)     *verb:* to be able to pay for (*can* or *can't* usually comes before **afford**)
    "We're not rich, but we can **afford** a new TV set."

## *Completing Sentences*

**Complete the sentences with these words.** *Use each word twice. Where a word has different endings, both forms are given.*

**neighbor/neighbors**          **of course**          **afford**          **expensive**

1. Florida is a great state to visit. _____ it's very hot in the summer.

2. These shoes are _____, but I'm going to buy them.

3. When I was in the hospital, many of my _____ came to see me.

4. It's a beautiful apartment. Do you think we can _____ the rent?

5. This is a gold watch. That's why it's _____ .

6. Jan lives near me, and I know he'll help me. He's a good _____ .

7. _____ we're hungry. It's 1:00, and we haven't eaten lunch yet.

8. Dan and Karen want to go to Hawaii, but they can't _____ it.

## *Creating Sentences*

**Write an original sentence using these words.** *Work with a partner or on your own.*

1. (of course) _____

   _____

2. (expensive) _____

   _____

3. (neighbor) _____

   _____

4. (afford) _____

   _____

# IV. MINI-DICTIONARY — PART TWO

## Vocabulary Focus

5. **choose** (chōōz)   *verb:* to take one thing from two or more; to pick; to select

   "The company is going to **choose** a new president."

   > The past tense of **choose** is **chose**.

6. **just** (just)   *adverb:* exactly*

   "Kyra looks **just** like her mother."

   *The adverb **just** has other meanings, for example, (a) *very recently*: "We **just** got home." (b) *only*: "I was **just** trying to help you."

7. **loan** (lōn)   *noun:* money or anything that a person is given and must pay or give back

   *verb:* to give money that must be paid back; to give anything that must be returned

   "Stacy went to the bank to ask for a **loan**.  She needs $3,000.

   "I'll **loan** the book to you.  I need it back."

8. **bor·row** (bor´ō *or* bôr´ō)   *verb*: to obtain money that must be paid back; to obtain or take anything that must be returned

   "May I **borrow** $30 from you?  I'll pay it back tomorrow."

## Completing Sentences

**Complete the sentences with these words.**  *Use each word twice.  Where a word has different endings, both forms are given.*

**borrowing/borrowed**          **just**          **loan/loaned**          **choose/chose**

1. The money I got from Scott wasn't a gift.  It was a _____ .

2. Steve _____ his cousin's car to drive to the airport.

3. Erica likes the college she _____ , and she's doing very well.

4. I asked Charley to write a report, and he did it _____ the way I wanted.

5. It's important to _____ friends carefully.

6. I _____ my bike to Art this morning; I hope he takes good care of it.

7. Your son and mine are _____ the same age.

8. I'm _____ Janet's typewriter, but I have to return it next week.

## Creating Sentences

**Write an original sentence using these words.** *Work with a partner or on your own.*

5. (choose) _____

_____

6. (just) _____

_____

7. (loan) _____

_____

8. (borrow) _____

_____

# V. STORY COMPLETION

**Discuss or think about these questions before completing the story that follows.**

1. How much experience do you have with computers?
2. Do you like working with them?
3. How expensive are home computers? How expensive are business computers?

**Complete the story with these words.**

| choose | loan | neighbors | borrow |
|--------|------|-----------|--------|
| expensive | afford | just | of course |

### Buying a Computer

Mr. Gonzalez and Mr. Fisher live on the same block. They're _____ and good friends. They also own an advertising business, and they want to buy a bigger and better computer for their business. _____ good business computers are _____, and there are so many different kinds that it's not easy to _____ the right one.

Yesterday they visited a computer store that sells IBM computers, and they were able to find one that is _____ right for their business. It does everything they want and is much faster than the one they have.

However, the only way they can _____ it is to _____ the money for it. They're going to a bank this afternoon to ask for a _____. They hope the bank will give them one.

## VI.   SHARING INFORMATION

**Discuss these questions and topics in pairs or small groups.**

1. Complete the following sentence: **Of course** I like (don't like) to _____ _____ , but _____ .

2. Name a store where you can buy clothing that's not **expensive**. Where can you eat out that's not expensive?

3. Are most of your **neighbors** friendly? How well do you know your neighbors? Do you think neighbors in other countries are friendlier than those in the United States?

4. Imagine that someone gave you a million dollars. What would you buy that you can't **afford** now?

5. If you had to **choose** between being very rich or very smart, what **choice** would you make?

6. Look at your watch or a clock and complete the following sentence: It's **just**

   _____.

7. Did you ever **loan** money to a friend or relative? Did you get it back?

8. Did you ever **borrow** money? Why did you borrow it? How much time did you have to pay it back?

# VII. WORD FAMILIES

**Complete the sentences with these words.** *If necessary, add an ending to the word so it forms a correct sentence.* (adj. = adjective and adv. = adverb)

1. **expensive** (adj.)          **expense** (noun)

   A. Food is a big _____ for all families.

   B. I love to travel, but it's _____.

2. **neighbor** (noun)     **neighborhood** (noun)     **neighboring** (adj.)

   A. It's a pretty _____ with tall trees and nice homes.

   B. Ralph is going to move his store to a _____ city.

   C. Mrs. Johnson sold her house. We'll be getting new _____.

3. **afford** (verb)          **affordable** (adj.)

   A. We want to buy a house, but it's hard to find one that's

   _____.

   B. That coat is beautiful, but I can't _____ it.

4. **choose** (verb)     **choice** (noun)

   A. I like the red sweater and the brown one. I don't know which one to

      _____ .

   B. We have to pay taxes. We have no _____ .

# VIII. BUILDING ADJECTIVES WITH -ABLE

The suffix **-able** is added to verbs and nouns to form an adjective. **-Able** usually means *able to be* or *likely to*. For example, *wash + able = washable*, which means *able to be washed; change + able = changeable*, which means *likely to change.*

**-Able** can also mean *having or giving*, for example, *value + able = valuable*, which means *having value; comfort + able = comfortable*, which means *giving comfort.*

| Verb or Noun | Adjective |
| --- | --- |
| accept | acceptable |
| afford | affordable |
| change | changeable |
| comfort | comfortable |
| control | controllable |
| enjoy | enjoyable |
| like | likable |
| pay | payable |
| return | returnable |
| understand | understandable |
| use | usable |
| value | valuable |
| wash | washable |
| work | workable |

**Circle the letter next to the word that *best* completes the sentence.**

1. Delia is very _____. You never know what's she going to do next.
   - a. valuable
   - b. changeable
   - c. unhealthy
   - d. knowledgeable

2. Everyone liked the show. It was _____.
   - a. controllable
   - b. usable
   - c. acceptable
   - d. enjoyable

3. These empty soda bottles are _____. We can bring them to the store

   and get money for them.
   - a. washable
   - b. affordable
   - c. returnable
   - d. likable

4. The teachers thought they had a good plan, but the principal said it wasn't

   _____.
   - a. acceptable
   - b. enjoyable
   - c. changeable
   - d. comfortable

5. The desk is big and heavy, but it's _____.
   - a. washable
   - b. likable
   - c. controllable
   - d. movable

6. The jacket is _____, but you should use warm water, not hot.
   - a. acceptable
   - b. washable
   - c. affordable
   - d. returnable

7. There was a fire in our apartment building. Fortunately, it was _____,

   and the firefighters put it out.
   - a. controllable
   - b. movable
   - c. workable
   - d. changeable

8. Jay's pay is low and he works long hours. His desire for a better job is

   _____.
   - a. knowledgeable
   - b. usable
   - c. understandable
   - d. acceptable

# IX.  READING CAR ADS

When Frank and Sue decided to buy a new car, they started to read the car ads in the newspaper.  But that wasn't easy.  The biggest problem was the large number of abbreviations in the ads.  Here are some they saw.

| Abbreviation | Meaning |
|---|---|
| 1. dr. | door |
| 2. cyl. or V | cylinder |
| 3. spd. | speed |
| 4. auto or auto trans. | automatic transmission |
| 5. man. or man. trans. | manual transmission |
| 6. air or a/c or air cond. | air conditioning |
| 7. P/S, P/B or p/s/b or psb | power steering and power brakes |
| 8. AM/FM st. cass. | AM/FM stereo cassette |
| 9. r/def. | rear defroster |
| 10. rdls. | radial tires |
| 11. VIN | vehicle identification number — This is used to identify the car on all paperwork. |
| 12. MSRP | manufacturer's suggested retail price — The price the manufacturer *suggests* to the dealer.  By law the price is placed on the window of all new cars. |
| 13. in stk. | in stock |

A.

> **New Ford Taurus**
>
> 4 DR, 6 CYL. AUTO, P/S/B,
>
> AIR, AM/FM ST., R. DEF.,
>
> VIN # CF 152719
>
> MSRP $14,755

1. Does this car have air conditioning?
2. What type of transmission does it have?
3. How many doors?

4. Does it have a rear defroster?

5. How many cylinders does it have?

6. Does it have a stereo radio?

7. Does it have a cassette player?

8. What does the ad tell you about the steering and brakes?

9. What's the car's identification number?

10. What's the price suggested by Ford?

**B.**

```
Used Cars

'90 Accord     $6,495

Honda 2-Dr.,  4-Cyl., 5-Spd.

Man.,  P/S/B, No Air, R/Def.,

A.M./F.M. St. Cass.,  Rdls.,

66,220 mi., VIN. GO 338192
```

1. Does this Accord have air conditioning?

2. How many doors does it have?

3. How many miles has it gone?

4. Does it have power steering and brakes?

5. How many cylinders does it have?

6. What kind of tires does it have?

7. Is the transmission automatic?

8. Does it have a cassette player?

9. What is its vehicle identification number?

10. Why doesn't the ad give an MSRP?

## Homework

Look at the car ads in the newspaper. Bring two of the ads to class. Copy one of them on the board, and ask another student in the class to read it.

# UNIT TWO WORD REVIEW

## I. SYNONYMS

Next to each sentence, write the word that has the same meaning or almost the same meaning as the part of the sentence in dark print.

| bit | fortunate | exploring | hates |
|-----|-----------|-----------|-------|
| just | burning | improving | both |

1. _____ The job pays well and I was **lucky** to get it.

2. _____ My dog **doesn't like** baths.

3. _____ Julio's car is **on fire.**

4. _____ Cristina put a **small amount** of milk and sugar in her tea.

5. _____ Doug is a good tennis player, and he's **getting better.**

6. _____ The baby weighs **exactly** 21 pounds.

7. _____ Marina and her sister are happy it's snowing. **The two** of them like to ski.

8. _____ The company is **looking carefully at** ways to cut expenses.

## II. SENTENCE COMPLETION

Complete the sentences with these words.

| choose | neighbors | swallow | share |
|--------|-----------|---------|-------|
| rushing | proud | wipe | poisonous |

1. Brad is late. He's _____ to get to class before the bell rings.

2. My bike got wet in the rain. I have to _____ it off.

3. This menu is so large and so good that I don't know what to _____ .

4. Kate is _____ of her beautiful garden.

5. Married couples _____ their lives.

6. Gale lives around the corner from us. We're _____ .

7. Many cleaning fluids and powders are _____ .

8. The soup was so hot that I couldn't _____ it.

# III. STORY COMPLETION

**Complete the story with these words.**

loan                    fun                         of course              still

mistake                 expensive                   borrow                 afford

### *A Boat*

Karl and Michelle are married and live in Dallas, Texas.  In the summer they

rent a home on a large lake because they like to get away from the heat of the city

and go swimming.  Now Karl wants to buy a boat, but Michelle says that boats are too

_____ and they can't _____ one.

Karl wants to _____ the money for the boat.  Michelle knows

they can get a _____ from the bank, but she

_____ doesn't like the idea.  She thinks it would be a

_____ to pay so much for something they don't need.

Karl says, "_____ we don't need a boat, but my business is

doing well, and it would be a lot of _____ to have one."

# UNIT THREE

# *Two Young Men*

# CHAPTER SEVEN
# *Working and Swimming*

??????????????????????????

## PREVIEW QUESTIONS

**Discuss or think about these questions before reading the story.**

1. Do you like to read? Do you like to study? Do you like school?

2. How interested are you in sports? What's your favorite sport?

3. Do you think high school students should work in the summer? Explain your answer. What kinds of jobs can they get?

# Working and Swimming

Pete and Tom are brothers. Pete's 18 and he'll graduate from high school in June. He's a good student and **spends** a lot of time reading and studying. Last year he had a B **average**, and this year he's getting all A's. Math is his favorite subject, but he also likes English and history. He plans to go to college in September and will have no trouble getting into a good one.

Tom's 16 and he hates school. He has only a C average, and he doesn't like to study or read. He **prefers** to play basketball and baseball or watch TV. He's good at all sports, especially basketball. Pete's shy and quiet and has only a few friends, but Tom likes to talk and has a lot of friends. Tom's also handsome, dresses well, and is a good dancer. He's very popular with the girls.

In the summer, Pete works at a gas station. He likes the work, especially when he gets the chance to fix cars. He loves cars and is learning a lot from the owner of the gas station, who's an excellent mechanic. Pete saves the money he makes to help pay for his college education. His parents aren't rich, and going to college is expensive.

Tom works at Burger King during the summer. "It's not great work," he says, "and I don't get paid much. But I'm happy to be working and making some money. It's not easy for a high school student to get a summer job." Some of Tom's friends don't work in the summer and don't want to. But he likes to work and he likes the money.

In the evening, Tom plays basketball in the park with his friends. It's not so hot then. Pete usually stays home and reads or watches TV, but sometimes he goes out with his friends. On Saturday and Sunday, Pete and Tom go swimming in a **pool** near their home. Pete's only an average swimmer, but Tom's very good.

They have to pay to get into the pool, but it's big and Pete and Tom have a lot of fun there. Tom likes to **dive** and swim in the **deep** end of the pool. Pete prefers to go in the **shallow** end. He can't dive well. They swim or sit on the **edge** of the pool until they get tired, and then they walk home. It's a nice way to spend a summer afternoon.

## I. COMPREHENSION QUESTIONS

**Answer these questions about the story.** *Use your judgment to answer questions with an asterisk(*). Work in pairs or small groups. The numbers in parentheses show which paragraph in the story has the answer.*

1. How does Pete spend much of his time? (1)

2. What does he plan to do in September? (1)

3. Name three things Tom likes to do. (2)

4. How are Pete and Tom different? (2)

75

*5. Are boys who are good at sports usually popular with girls?  If so, why?

6. What does Pete like to do at the gas station?  (3)

7. Why is he learning a lot from the owner of the gas station?  (3)

*8. Do you think Pete can get financial aid to go to college?  If so, why?  And how?

9. Why is Tom happy to be working?  Give two reasons.  (4)

10. What do Pete and Tom do on Saturday and Sunday?  (5)

11. What end of the pool does Tom like to go in?  And Pete?  (6)

*12. Who do you think has more fun at the pool, Tom or Pete?  Explain your answer.

# II.  WORD GUESSING

**Guess the meaning of the key words in these sentences.**  *Use the context of the story and the sentences to guess.  Circle your answers.*

1. Pete is a good student and **spends** *a lot of time* reading and studying.

   a. wastes a lot of time          c. doesn't like

   b. enjoys                        d. uses a lot of time

2. Pete **prefers** to play basketball and baseball or watch TV.

   a. has to                        c. tries to

   b. likes to…better               d. is afraid to

3. Tom likes to **dive** and swim in the deep end of the pool.

   a. jump head first into the water     c. run into the water

   b. walk quickly into the water        d. walk slowly into the water

# III.  MINI-DICTIONARY — PART ONE

## *Vocabulary Focus*

1. **spend** (spend)     *verb*:  A.  to use money to buy something

                                  B.  to use time

   "Clara **spends** a lot of money on clothes."

   "Fran **spent** 40 minutes washing his car."

                        The past of **spend** is **spent**.

76

2. **av·er·age** (av´rij)    *adjective*: ordinary

*noun*: the result of adding several numbers and then dividing by how many numbers were added
(4 + 5 + 6 = 15; 15 ÷ 3 = 5)

*verb*:  A.  to do on average

B.  to add and divide to get an average

"Lisa is an **average** cook.  She's not great and she's not bad."

"I got 65, 85, and 90 on my tests this marking period.  My **average** is 80."

"We **averaged** 55 miles an hour on our trip to Virginia."

3. **pre·fer** (pri-fûr´)    *verb*:  to like better

"Sometimes I drink tea, but I **prefer** coffee."

4. **pool** (pool)    *noun*:  A.  a small area of water

B.  a small area of water for swimming

"The rain was heavy, and **pools** of water are on the field."

"I want to stay at a motel that has a **pool**."

## Completing Sentences

**Complete the sentences with these words.**  *Use each word twice.  Where a word has different endings, both forms are given.*

| average/averaging | spending/spent | pool | prefer/prefers |
|---|---|---|---|

1. Joyce _____ $60 at the supermarket.

2. I like to go to the movies, but my wife _____ to stay home and

   watch TV.

3. Doris isn't your _____ lawyer.  She's one of the best.

4. There's a _____ of water on the bathroom floor.

5. We can fly to Chicago or go by train.  Which do you _____?

6. I hear our new high school is going to have a _____.  That's great!

7. Eric is _____ the evening at his friend's house.

8. Tom is the best basketball player on his team.  He's _____ 20 points

   a game.

## Creating Sentences

**Write an original sentence using these words.** *Work with a partner or on your own.*

1. (spend) _____

2. (average) _____

3. (prefer) _____

4. (pool) _____

# IV.  MINI-DICTIONARY — PART TWO

## Vocabulary Focus

5. **dive** (dīv)    *verb*: to jump head first into water

                        *noun*:  a head-first jump into water

    "Keith is **diving** into the river."

    "Pam made a beautiful **dive** into the pool."

              The past of **dive** is **dived** or **dove**.

6. **deep** (dēp)    *adjective*: going far down or into

                 *adverb*:  far down or into

    "The middle of the lake is very **deep**."

    "The U.S. army moved **deep** into Iraq."

7. **shal·low** (shalʹō)    *adjective*: not far from top to bottom; not deep

    "It's all right for the baby to go into the pool.  It's very **shallow**."

8. **edge** (ej)    *noun*: the area where an object ends

    "Oscar is sitting on the **edge** of the bed, putting on his shoes."

## Completing Sentences

**Complete the sentences with these words.** *Use each word twice.  Where a word has different endings, both forms are given.*

| shallow | dive/diving | edge | deep |
| --- | --- | --- | --- |

1. Alex is afraid to _____ into the water.  He can't swim well.

2. That's a very _____ cut.  I'm taking you to the hospital.

3. The books fell off the _____ of the desk.

4. The road is covered with water, but it's _____.  We can drive

   through it.

5. We don't always understand Eileen.  She's a _____ thinker.

6. You're driving too close to the _____ of the road.

7. Abdul is _____ into the ocean.

8. The lake is small, and it's too _____ to swim in.

## *Creating Sentences*

**Write an original sentence using these words.**  *Work with a partner or on your own.*

5. (dive) _____

6. (deep) _____

7. (shallow) _____

8. (edge) _____

# V.  STORY COMPLETION

**Discuss or think about these questions before completing the story that follows.**

1. Can you swim?  Are you a good swimmer?
2. Do you swim much?  Where do you swim?
3. Why is it good to know how to swim?

**Complete the story with these words.**

edge        shallow        spend        dive

deep        prefer        average        pool

## *Swimming in the River*

Ruth and her brother Todd like to swim. Sometimes they go to a state park where there is a _____, but they have to drive ten miles to get there. They _____ to swim in a river near their house. They can walk there in five minutes.

They like to _____ into the water from the _____ of the river and swim until it's time to go home. In July and August, when the weather is hot and the days are long, they _____ hours swimming in the cool water.

Although the river is _____ where they go swimming, they aren't afraid. Ruth is an excellent swimmer, and Todd is above _____. Parts of the river are _____ and very safe, but they don't like to swim there. It's not as much fun.

# VI. SHARING INFORMATION

**Discuss these questions and topics in pairs or small groups.**

1. Do you **spend** a lot of time watching TV? Talking on the phone? Reading?
2. Are you tall or short? Or is your height **average**?
3. Complete this sentence: I like _____, but I **prefer** _____.
4. Do you think it's more fun to swim in the ocean or in a **pool**? Why? Which is safer?

5. **Divers** explore the ocean, and some of them look for ships that are at the bottom of the ocean. What famous ship did divers find in the Atlantic Ocean in 1989? The name of the ship begins with a *T*.

6. Most people have a **deep** interest in something, for example, politics, movies, clothes, sports, history. Name something you're **deeply** interested in.

7. Abraham Lincoln was a deep thinker. What does that mean? What do we mean when we say that a person is a **shallow** thinker?

8. Many people are afraid to stand near the **edge** of a high roof or bridge. They're afraid of heights. Are you?

# VII. WORD FAMILIES

**Complete the sentences with these words.** *If necessary, add an ending to the word so it forms a correct sentence.* (adj. = adjective and adv. = adverb)

1. **prefer** (verb)      **preference** (noun)      **preferable** (adj.)

    A. If you have the money, buying a house is usually _____ to renting.

    B. I like country music, but my son _____ rock.

    C. We have vanilla, chocolate, and strawberry ice cream. What's your

    _____?

2. **dive** (verb)      **diver** (noun)

    A. I love to watch the _____ in the Olympic Games.

    B. It's not safe to _____ into this pool. It's too shallow.

3. **deep** (adj. or adv.)      **deeply** (adv.)
   **deepen** (verb)      **depth** (noun)

    A. What is the _____ of the river?

    B. Pedro and Lynn are _____ in love.

    C. They're going to _____ the lake so people can swim in it.

    D. The trunk of the car is _____ . We can get a lot in it.

# VIII. BUILDING ADJECTIVES AND NOUNS WITH -FUL

The suffix **-ful** is added to nouns to form an adjective. For example, *power + ful = powerful*; *beauty + ful = beautiful*; *help + ful = helpful*.

**-Ful** usually means *full* or *having a lot of*, or *giving*. *Powerful* means *full of power*; *beautiful* means *having a lot of beauty*; *helpful* means *giving help*.

Sometimes -ful is added to a noun to form another noun. For example, *spoon + ful = spoonful*; *arm + ful = armful*. In these cases, **-ful** means *the amount that makes the thing full*. *Spoonful* means *the amount that makes a spoon full*; *armful* means *the amount that makes an arm full*.

| Noun | Adjective |
|---|---|
| beauty | beautiful |
| care | careful |
| color | colorful |
| fear | fearful |
| help | helpful |
| hope | hopeful |
| joy | joyful |
| peace | peaceful |
| power | powerful |
| rest | restful |
| thought | thoughtful |
| use | useful |
| waste | wasteful |
| youth | youthful |

| | **Noun** |
|---|---|
| arm | armful |
| spoon | spoonful |

**Circle the letter next to the word that *best* completes the sentence.**

1. The book was very _____. It helped a lot.
   - a. fearful
   - b. useful
   - c. colorful
   - d. youthful

2. Lillian never drives fast. She's a _____ driver.
   - a. joyful
   - b. powerful
   - c. peaceful
   - d. careful

3. Thinking about war and nuclear bombs makes us _____.
   - a. fearful
   - b. useful
   - c. powerful
   - d. restful

4. It's _____ to cook more than you'll eat.
   - a. thoughtful
   - b. helpful
   - c. wasteful
   - d. colorful

5. Life in the country is more _____ than life in the city.
   - a. useful
   - b. careful
   - c. powerful
   - d. peaceful

6. I'm not sure I'll get the job, but I'm _____.
   - a. hopeful
   - b. colorful
   - c. thoughtful
   - d. helpful

7. Greg is 40, but he's still _____.
   - a. careful
   - b. fearful
   - c. youthful
   - d. wasteful

8. It's fall and the leaves on the trees are _____.
   - a. powerful
   - b. colorful
   - c. helpful
   - d. useful

# CHAPTER EIGHT
# *Hunting*

# PREVIEW QUESTIONS

**Discuss or think about these questions before reading the story.**

1. Some people think it's okay to hunt. Others say it's wrong to kill animals for sport. What do you think? Explain your answer.

2. Did you ever hunt? Do you know anyone who likes to hunt?

3. Why do people like to hunt?

# *Hunting*

Pete and Tom hate to see the summer end. The day after Labor Day,* the pool closes and they have to go back to school. That's no fun. It's especially hard on Tom, but Pete also misses the pool and his work at the gas station.

There's one thing that Pete and Tom do like about the fall. They love to **hunt**. When Tom was in the eighth grade and Pete was in high school, their father taught them how to hunt. But their mother didn't like the idea one bit. "I don't think anyone should **shoot** animals," she said. "Killing is never right." And of course she was also afraid that her sons might get hurt. She still tells them to be careful when they go hunting.

On Saturdays in the fall, Pete and Tom get up at 6:00 and spend the day hunting. Their father owns a small Ford truck, and he lets them borrow it to drive to the woods around 20 miles from their house. The woods are a great place to hunt, and they are especially beautiful when the leaves change colors in the fall.

Last Saturday Pete and Tom were walking in the woods with their rifles when they saw a deer drinking from a **stream**. They were hunting for rabbits and were surprised and happy to see the deer. It was almost too beautiful to shoot. They moved closer. They **hesitated** for a minute. Should they shoot the deer or let it go? Then Tom **aimed** his rifle at the deer and shot. Tom's aim is very good; he didn't miss.

This was the first time they ever shot a deer. They were happy and sad at the same time. They remembered their mother's words about killing. They went over to the deer. It was a **huge** animal. They tried to **lift** it, but it was too heavy. They had to **drag** it on the ground to their truck; it wasn't far.

Some **hunters** helped them lift the deer into the truck. They put their rifles next to the deer and started home. "I can't wait to show the deer to Dad," Tom said. "He'll think we're great hunters."

---

*\*Labor Day** is a national holiday in the United States. It honors working men and women and is celebrated on the first Monday of September.

# I.  COMPREHENSION QUESTIONS

## *True or False*

**If the sentence is true, write *T*.  If it's false, write *F* and change it to a true statement.**

_____ 1. Tom and Pete go back to school on Labor Day.

_____

_____ 2. It's especially hard for Tom to return to school.

_____

_____ 3. Pete and Tom's mother was happy that they learned to hunt.

_____

_____ 4. On Saturdays in the fall, Pete and Tom get up early to go hunting.

_____

_____ 5. Their father drives them to the woods.

_____

_____ 6. Pete and Tom were surprised and happy to see the deer.

_____

_____ 7. Tom shot the deer immediately.

_____

_____ 8. Some hunters helped lift the deer into the truck.

_____

## What Do You Think?

**Use your experience, judgment, and the story to answer these questions.** *The story alone won't answer them.*

1. Why was going back to school especially hard on Tom?

2. Sometimes hunters accidentally shoot other hunters. What can hunters do to protect themselves?

3. Why were Pete and Tom happy that they shot the deer? Why do you think they were also sad?

4. What do you think their father said when he saw the deer? And their mother?

# II.  WORD GUESSING

**Guess the meaning of the key words in these sentences.** *Use the context of the story and the sentences to guess.* *Circle your answers.*

1. Pete and Tom loved to **hunt**.

   a. feed animals

   b. take pictures of animals

   c. look for animals to kill or capture

   d. watch animals

2. Pete and Tom moved closer to the deer. They **hesitated** for a minute.

   a. talked

   b. were happy

   c. were quiet

   d. stopped

3. Pete and Tom went over to the deer. It was a **huge** animal.

   a. very beautiful

   b. very large

   c. very nice

   d. very small

# III. MINI-DICTIONARY — PART ONE

## *Vocabulary Focus*

1. a. **hunt** (hunt)  *verb*:  A.  to look for animals to kill or capture
   B.  to look carefully for anything
   *noun*:  the act of hunting

   "Victor and his cousin John like to **hunt** ducks."

   "Peggy is **hunting** for a job."

   "Warren is going to a **hunt**.  That's why he has a rifle in the trunk of his car."

   b. **hun·ter** (hun´tər)  *noun*:  a person who hunts

   "The fox is running away from the **hunters** and the dogs."

2. **shoot** (shoot)  *verb*:  to hit, or try to hit, with a bullet from a gun

   "The man who robbed the bank had a gun in his hand, but he didn't **shoot** anyone."

   The past of **shoot** is **shot**.

3. **stream** (strēm)  *noun*:  A.  a body of water that flows, especially a small one
   B.  anything that flows continuously
   *verb*:  to flow continuously

   "We sat on the side of the **stream** and put our feet into the water."

   "It was 5:00 P.M., and a **stream** of people was coming out of the train station."

   "Water was **streaming** from the broken pipe."

4. **hes·i·tate** (hez´ə-tāt)  *verb*:  A.  to stop briefly before or during an action
   B.  to be slow or unwilling to act or decide

   "Nick **hesitated** before he answered my question."

   "I **hesitated** to phone my friend.  It was very late."

88

## Completing Sentences

**Complete the sentences with these words.** *Use each word twice. Where a word has different endings, both forms are given.*

**stream**          **hesitates/hesitated**          **hunt/hunting**          **shoot/shot**

1. I _____ to ask my sister for a loan, but I needed the money.

2. Lee Harvey Oswald _____ President John Kennedy in Dallas, Texas, on November 22, 1963.

3. There are no fish in the _____ . It's too shallow.

4. You need a license to _____ .

5. The soldier told the man to stop, or he would _____ .

6. Melissa thinks her salary is much too low, but she _____ to quit her job.

7. Kevin and Pat are _____ for an apartment. They want to move.

8. It's 3:00, and a _____ of students is coming out of school.

## Creating Sentences

**Write an original sentence using these words.** *Work with a partner or on your own.*

1. (hunt) _____

   _____

2. (shoot) _____

   _____

3. (stream) _____

   _____

4. (hesitate) _____

   _____

# IV.  MINI-DICTIONARY — PART TWO

5. **aim** (ām)   *verb*: A.  to point a gun or other thing at a person or object
    B.  to plan to do something
    *noun*: A.  the act of aiming
    B.  what one wishes to do; a plan

   "The soldier **aimed** his rifle at the enemy."

   "Our company **aims** to make more money next year."

   "Police officers practice shooting to improve their **aim**."

   "What are the **aims** of the president's trip to Europe?"

6. **huge** (hyōōj *or* yōōj)   *adjective*: very large

   "Lake Champlain is 121 miles long.  It's **huge**."

7. **lift** (lift)   *verb*: to raise something to a higher position
    *noun*: the act of lifting

   "I want to move this desk.  Can you help me **lift** it?"

   "I gave the little boy a **lift** over the fence.  He wanted to get his ball."

8. **drag** (drag)   *verb*: to pull along on a surface

   "Beverly is **dragging** a big box out of the closet."

## *Completing Sentences*

**Complete the sentences with these words.**  *Use each word twice.  Where a word has different endings, both forms are given.*

| lift/lifts | drag/dragging | huge | aim/aims |
|---|---|---|---|

1. One of the _____ of the space program was to land an astronaut on

   the moon.

2. The baby is _____ her doll behind her.

3. There are many _____ buildings in Chicago.

4. The suitcases are light.  They'll  be easy to _____.

5. Canada is larger than the United States.  It's a _____ country.

6. I told my son I would _____ him out of bed if he didn't get up soon.

7. Kareem is strong. He _____ weights every day.

8. My brother and I own a clothing store, and we _____ to please our customers.

### Creating Sentences

**Write an original sentence using these words.** *Work with a partner or on your own.*

5. (aim) _____

_____

6. (huge) _____

_____

7. (lift) _____

_____

8. (drag) _____

_____

## V.   STORY COMPLETION

**Discuss or think about these questions before completing the story that follows.**

1. Did you ever go camping? Would you like to?
2. Did you ever see a bear other than in a zoo or circus? If so, where?
3. Many bears look friendly. Is it safe to feed or go near them? Explain your answer.

**Complete the story with these words.**

huge          dragged          hunt          aim

shot          hesitate          lift          stream

### A Hungry Bear

Scott, Lisa, and their two children love the outdoors.  One summer they were camping near a _____ in Acadia National Park in Maine.  No one is allowed to _____ in the park, but Scott had his rifle with him.  He never thought he would have to use it, but he felt safer with it.

Their youngest child, Jessica, was playing outside their tent when a _____ bear came looking for food.  Scott got his rifle, and when he saw the bear running toward Jessica, he didn't _____ a moment.  Fortunately, Scott has a good _____.  He _____ and killed the bear.

Jessica ran into the tent crying.  Her mother hugged her and told her everything was okay.  Scott went over to the bear.  It was too heavy to _____, so they _____ it away from the tent and left it under a tree.

## VI.   SHARING INFORMATION

**Discuss these questions and topics in pairs or small groups.**

1. Laws limit when people can **hunt** and the number of animals a **hunter** can kill.  Do you think the government should do more to limit hunting and protect animals?  Explain your answer.

2. Thousands of people are **shot** and killed in the United States every year.  Do you think we need stricter laws to control guns?  Explain your answer.

3. The word **stream** usually refers to water, but it can also refer to other things, for example, a stream of people or a stream of questions.  What do we mean by a stream of people?  A stream of questions?

4. Complete sentence A or B:  A.  I **hesitated** to _____

_____ .  B.  I **hesitated** before _____ .

5. Everyone needs to have **aims**, things they plan or are trying to do.  Name one of your aims.  Why are aims so important in life?

6. There are many problems in the world.  Some are small; others are **huge**.  Name one of the huge ones.

7. Name some things that are heavy and difficult to **lift**.  Name some that are light and easy to lift.

8. When time seems to move slowly, we say it **drags**.  Does time ever drag for you?  If so, when?

# VII.  WORD FAMILIES

**Complete the sentences with these words.**  *If necessary, add an ending to the word so it forms a correct sentence.*  (adj. = adjective and adv. = adverb)

1. **hunt** (noun or verb)          **hunter** (noun)          **hunting** (noun)

   A. _____ get a lot of fresh air and exercise.

   B. _____ and fishing are popular sports.

   C. Most African countries don't allow anyone to _____ elephants.

2. **shoot** (verb)          **shot** (noun)

   A. When I saw that the man had a gun, I said, "Take my watch and wallet, but

      don't _____ ."

   B. Someone tried to kill Henry, but the _____ missed.

3. **hesitate** (verb)          **hesitant** (adj.)
   **hesitantly** (adv.)          **hesitation** (noun)

   A. Ashley _____ told her father about the auto accident she was in.

   B. We _____ to go swimming; the water was cold.

   *C. I have a new battery in my car, and it starts without _____ .

   D. We knew Irene's son was taking drugs, but we were _____ to tell her.

      *There are two possible answers to C.

93

# VIII. BUILDING ADJECTIVES WITH -LESS

The suffix **-less** is added to nouns to form an adjective. For example, *power + less = powerless; fear + less = fearless.*

The suffix **-less** means *having no* or *without*. *Powerless* means *having no power* or *without power; fearless* means *having no fear* or *without fear.*

| Noun | Adjective | Noun | Adjective |
|------|-----------|------|-----------|
| aim | aimless | need | needless |
| care | careless | power | powerless |
| end | endless | sleep | sleepless |
| fear | fearless | speech | speechless |
| help | helpless | sugar | sugarless |
| home | homeless | use | useless |
| hope | hopeless | weight | weightless |

**Circle the letter next to the word that *best* completes the sentence.**

1. I buy _____ gum. It's better for my teeth.
   - a. weightless
   - b. sugarless
   - c. useless
   - d. powerless

2. Fred made some _____ mistakes on his math exam.
   - a. hopeless
   - b. aimless
   - c. fearless
   - d. careless

3. Denise is very tired. She had a (an) _____ night.
   - a. endless
   - b. useless
   - c. sleepless
   - d. speechless

4. Does the city have a place where _____ people can stay?
   - a. homeless
   - b. careless
   - c. powerless
   - d. aimless

5. The movie was too long. It seemed _____.
   - a. hopeless
   - b. useless
   - c. endless
   - d. helpless

6. Jesse will make a good soldier. He's _____.

    a. careless            c. weightless

    b. fearless            d. aimless

7. This clock is _____. It won't run.

    a. needless           c. endless

    b. helpless           d. useless

8. Everything in outerspace is _____.

    a. weightless        c. powerless

    b. aimless          d. speechless

# CHAPTER NINE
# *A Bitter Argument*

## PREVIEW QUESTIONS

**Discuss or think about these questions before reading the story.**

1. Many students leave high school before they graduate. We say they drop out of school. Is it easy or difficult for these students to get good jobs? Explain your answer.

2. Why do students drop out of school?

3. What can high schools do to help students stay in school and graduate? What can parents do?

# A Bitter Argument

Tom and Pete live in New York State, where you have to go to school until you're 16. Then you're free to **quit** or to continue. Tom's just 16 and he wants to quit and go to work. However, his teachers and counselor know that to get a good job, he should **at least** finish high school. They want him to stay in school and to graduate.

Tom likes his science class, but he thinks that all of his other classes are a waste of time. He feels they're **dull** and that he's not learning anything in them. His teachers say that he's a nice boy, but that he's lazy and doesn't study. He says he doesn't want to study. He wants to get a job and **earn** some money. "Why does everyone have to go to school and study?" he asks. "Thomas Edison* never finished the first grade, and he did all right for himself."

Tom's parents also want him to stay in school. They think it would be **foolish** for him to quit. "All of the other boys and girls in the neighborhood plan to finish high school," his mother said to him. "And no one is going to give you a good job if you don't have a high school diploma. You're no Tom Edison. Why don't you finish high school and then look for a job?"

Tom doesn't care what the other kids are doing. "I want to be myself, and I want to go to work now," he said to his mother. "Look, I'm 16 and I'm not a baby anymore. You have to let me grow up. You know I hate school."

"I know," she replied, "that there are a lot of things in life that we hate and that we have to do. If you quit school now, you're running away from your problem, and that's no way to grow up."

Last night, Tom and his mother had another **argument** about his plan to quit school. She **shouted** at him and he shouted back at her. They **argued** for more than an hour. She said he would be a **fool** to quit school. He said he didn't want to hear any more about school and what his friends were doing. It was a **bitter** argument. Will Tom listen to his mother, or will he quit school?

---

*Thomas Edison was a famous inventor. He left school in the first grade. However, his mother was a teacher and she taught him at home. He also read a lot.

# I. COMPREHENSION QUESTIONS

**Answer these questions about the story.** *Use your judgment to answer questions with an asterisk(*). Work in pairs or small groups. The numbers in parentheses show which paragraph in the story has the answer.*

1. At what age can you quit school in New York? (1)

2. Why do Tom's teachers and counselor want him to stay in school? (1)

*3. Why do you think Tom likes his science class?

4. Why does he think that most of his classes are a waste of time?  (2)

*5. What do you think makes a class dull?   What makes one interesting?

6. What do Tom's teachers say about him?  (2)

7. What do his parents think of his quitting school?  (3)

8. What does his mother say about the other boys and girls in the neighborhood?  (3)

9. What does Tom say he wants?  (4)

10. How does his mother reply?  (5)

11. What did Tom and his mother argue about last night?  (6)

*12. Do you think he'll listen to his mother, or will he quit school?  Explain your answer.

# II.   WORD GUESSING

**Guess the meaning of the key words in these sentences.**  *Use the context of the story and the sentences to guess.  Circle your answers.*

1. Tom's parents think it would be **foolish** for him to quit.

    a.  a good idea          c.  necessary

    b.  stupid          d.  preferable

2. Tom's mother **shouted** *at him,* and he shouted back at her.

    a.  spoke to him in a loud voice      c.  spoke to him in a quiet voice

    b.  corrected him      d.  laughed at him

3. It was a **bitter** argument.

    a.  long          c.  friendly

    b.  very interesting          d.  very unpleasant

# III.   MINI-DICTIONARY — PART ONE

## *Vocabulary Focus*

1. **quit** (kwit)     *verb:* to stop doing something

"I know smoking is a bad habit, but it's difficult to **quit**."

The past of **quit** is **quit**.

98

2. **at least** (at lēst)    *idiom*: A. a minimum; maybe more, but not less

B. in any case

"A new refrigerator will cost **at least** $300."

"Our new boss is strict, but **at least** she listens."

3. **dull** (dul)    *adjective*: A. not interesting

B. not sharp

"I didn't finish the book. It was **dull**."

"These knives are **dull**. They won't cut the steak."

4. **earn** (ûrn)    *verb*: A. to receive money for doing work

B. to receive something because of one's actions or qualities

"Luz has a good job. She **earns** $65,000 a year."

"Our history teacher gives good marks only to those who **earn** them."

## Completing Sentences

**Complete the sentences with these words.** *Use each word twice. Where a word has different endings, both forms are given.*

**dull**              **at least**              **earn/earned**              **quit/quits**

1. I was going ———————— 70 miles an hour when the police officer stopped me.

2. Audrey never ———————— trying. She'll do well in life.

3. We left before the end of the game. It was ————————.

4. Most doctors ———————— a lot of money.

5. Jeff ———————— the baseball team. He wasn't playing much, and he didn't

   like the coach.

6. These scissors are ————————. I'm going to buy a better pair.

7. It was cloudy the day we had our picnic, but ———————— it didn't rain.

8. The soldiers fought bravely. They ———————— their medals.

99

## Creating Sentences

**Write an original sentence using these words.** *Work with a partner or on your own.*

1. (quit) _____

_____

2. (at least) _____

_____

3. (dull) _____

_____

4. (earn) _____

_____

# IV. MINI-DICTIONARY — PART TWO

## Vocabulary Focus

5. a. **fool** (fo͞ol)   *noun*: a stupid person

   *verb*: A. to trick; to make a person think something is true when it's not

   B. to joke; to kid

   "Donna was a **fool** to marry Lee. He's lazy and he drinks too much."

   "We thought Mickey was telling the truth, but he wasn't. He **fooled** us."

   "Valerie wasn't serious; she was only **fooling**."

   b. **fool·ish** (fo͞ol´ish)   *adjective*: stupid; not wise

   "It's **foolish** to go to work when you're sick."

6. a. **ar·gue** (är´gyo͞o)   *verb*: to fight with words; to disagree

   "Michelle and Brendan **argue** a lot about politics. She's a Democrat and he's a Republican."

   b. **ar·gu·ment** (är´gyə-mənt)   *noun*: a fight with words; a disagreement

   "Shawn likes to save money, and his wife likes to spend it. This causes a lot of **arguments**."

100

7. **shout** (shout)    *verb*: to speak in a very loud voice

                        *noun*: a loud cry

"You don't have to **shout**. I can hear you."

"We heard a **shout** in the hall and went to see what was happening."

8. **bit·ter** (bit´ər)    *adjective*: A. having a sharp, unpleasant taste

                                B. filled with strong, unpleasant feelings

"I never chew aspirin. It tastes **bitter**."

"Larry and Reggie had a **bitter** fight, and they're no longer friends."

## *Completing Sentences*

**Complete the sentences with these words.** *Use each word twice. Where a word has different endings, both forms are given.*

| argue/argument | bitter | fool/foolish | shout/shouts |
|---|---|---|---|

1. The lemonade is ——————————. Put some sugar in it.

2. When the class gets noisy, our teacher —————————— at us.

3. Just do what you're told and don't ——————————.

4. We were —————————— to buy a used car. We've had a lot of problems with it.

5. There was an accident in the parking lot, and the drivers got into a (an)

   ——————————.

6. Today the United States and Germany are good friends, but in World War II they

   were —————————— enemies.

7. I came quickly when I heard a —————————— for help.

8. You would be a —————————— to believe everything you read in that

   newspaper.

## Creating Sentences

**Write an original sentence using these words.** *Work with a partner or on your own.*

5. (foolish) _____

_____

6. (argue) _____

_____

7. (shout) _____

_____

8. (bitter) _____

_____

# V.  STORY COMPLETION

**Discuss or think about these questions before completing the story that follows.**
1. Why is work in a factory dull?
2. Why is the pay low?
3. Why do factories today need fewer workers?

### Complete the story with these words.

| | | | |
|---|---|---|---|
| earn | bitter | shout | at least |
| dull | quit | argument | foolish |

### Working in a Factory

Jerry works in a pencil factory, and his job is very _____. He does the same thing every day. The factory is also dirty, and the machines make a lot of noise. If Jerry wants to talk to another worker, he has to _____.

The biggest problem, however, is that Jerry's pay is low. Naturally, he wants to _____ more money.

Last month, Jerry and his boss had a long _____ about his salary. He told the boss that he never misses work and that his pay was too low. His boss promised to pay him more, but now he says it's impossible. Jerry is _____ about this. A promise is a promise, he says.

Jerry thinks it would be _____ to keep working in the factory. He's not going to get more money, and he doesn't trust his boss anymore. Tomorrow he's going to _____ his job and look for one that pays _____ $8 an hour.

# VI.  SHARING INFORMATION

**Discuss these questions and topics in pairs or small groups.**

1. Why do people **quit** their jobs?  Give as many reasons as you can.

2. Complete the following sentences:  A. A new small car, for example, a Ford Escort, costs **at least** _____ dollars.  B. I'm **at least** _____ feet _____ inches tall.

3. Some things we do are **dull** and some are interesting.  Complete these sentences: _____ is dull. _____ is interesting.

4. In the area where you live, what do you think the average factory worker **earns** in a year?  The average secretary?  The average teacher?  The average doctor?

5. Name some things that people do that are **foolish**, for example, drinking too much, driving too fast.

6. People **argue** about politics, sports, and many other things.  Tell us something you argue about.  Who do you argue with?  Friends?  Parents?  Husband?  Wife?

7. Why do parents **shout** at their children?  Do you think it's a good way to get them to listen and do what they're told?  Explain your answer.

8. Name as many things as you can that taste **bitter**.

# VII. WORD FAMILIES

**Complete the sentences with these words.** *If necessary, add an ending to the word so it forms a correct sentence.* (adj. = adjective and adv. = adverb)

1. **earn** (verb)                    **earnings** (noun)

   A. The government taxes our _____.

   B. Major league baseball players _____ a lot of money.

2. **fool** (noun or verb)            **foolish** (adj.)
   **foolishly** (adv.)               **foolishness** (noun)

   A. Someone took the packages we _____ left in our car.

   B. It's hard to _____ Stacy.   She's very smart.

   C. Erin hasn't been feeling well, but she won't go to the doctor.

      What _____!

   D. Ernie had a lot to drink at the party.  He was _____ to drive home.

3. **bitter** (adj.)            **bitterly** (adv.)            **bitterness** (noun)

   A. Terry cried _____ when her husband died.

   B. Our basketball team lost a big game by one point.  It was a

      _____ loss.

   C. There was much _____ in the African-American community after

      the shooting of Martin Luther King, Jr.

# VIII.   BUILDING NOUNS WITH -NESS

The suffix **-ness** is added to adjectives to form a noun.  For example, *weak + ness = weakness; kind + ness = kindness.*

**-Ness** means *the condition of being* or *the quality of being.  Weakness* means *the condition of being weak;  kindness* means *the quality of being kind.*

| Adjective | Noun | Adjective | Noun |
|-----------|------|-----------|------|
| bitter | bitterness | happy | happiness |
| careless | carelessness | kind | kindness |
| dark | darkness | sad | sadness |
| foolish | foolishness | serious | seriousness |
| friendly | friendliness | sick | sickness |
| good | goodness | soft | softness |
| great | greatness | weak | weakness |

**Circle the letter next to the word that *best* completes the sentence.**

1.  Does the president understand the _____ of the problem?
    - a. sadness
    - b. darkness
    - c. seriousness
    - d. sickness

2.  Sarah often eats too much.  It's a _____ of hers.
    - a. greatness
    - b. weakness
    - c. carelessness
    - d. happiness

3.  Many people like Dennis because of his _____.
    - a. softness
    - b. sadness
    - c. friendliness
    - d. bitterness

4.  Everyone is looking for _____.
    - a. happiness
    - b. seriousness
    - c. softness
    - d. greatness

5.  We couldn't see the house because of the _____.
    - a. carelessness
    - b. darkness
    - c. bitterness
    - d. foolishness

6. I like the warmth and _____ of the blanket.

    a. greatness           c. friendliness

    b. seriousness        d. softness

7. It's easy to ask Elsie for help because of her _____.

    a. kindness            c. sadness

    b. happiness         d. foolishness

8. The fire was started by the _____ of a smoker.

    a. weakness          c. friendliness

    b. bitterness          d. carelessness

# IX. READING HELP-WANTED ADS

Tom wanted to quit school and go to work to earn money. That's why he read the Help-Wanted ads in the newspapers. Here are some of the ads and abbreviations he read.

| Abbreviation | Meaning |
|---|---|
| 1. exp. or exper. | experience; experienced |
| 2. req. | required (necessary) |
| 3. hr. - wk. - mo. | hour - week - month |
| 4. P/T  F/T | part/time   full/time |
| 5. M/F | male/female |
| 6. excel. or exc. | excellent |
| 7. bnfts. | benefits |
| 8. neg. | negotiable |
| 9. avail. | available |
| 10. info. | information |
| 11. HSD | high school diploma |
| 12. GED | high school equivalency diploma |
| 13. lic. | license |
| 14. ext. | extension |

A.
> **Auto Mechanic**
> Exper. mechanic wanted. Must
> have driver's lic. Salary neg.
> Excel. bnfts. Call 212-823-3131.
> Ask for Max.

1.  What two things do you need for this job?
2.  What will your salary be?
3.  What kind of benefits does the ad say you will get?
4.  Who are you going to talk with about the job?

B.
> **Airline Now Hiring**
> Many entry-level positions.
> Top pay. 18 years or older.
> HSD/GED req. 1-800-441-6239

1.  Do you need a college education for these jobs? How much education do you need?
2.  How old must you be?
3.  Do you need experience?
4. Who will pay for a phone call to ask about the jobs?

C.

> **Salad Chef  M/F**
> Wash, peel, cut, and mix
> vegetables for potato and
> green salads.  3 mos. exp.,
> $8 per hr., 40 hrs. per wk.,
> 11 am – 8 pm with 1 hr. break.
> 201-472-9605

1. Is this job open to men and women?  How do you know?
2. How much experience do you need?
3. How much do you get per hour?  Per week?
4. How many days a week do you work?
5. Do you get paid for your break?

D.

> **Waiters/Waitresses  FT/PT**
> All shifts avail.  Great pay,
> excel. bnfts.  Apply in person,
> Billy's Diner.  906 Valley Rd.,
> Paterson, N.J.

1. Are these full-time or part-time jobs?  Or are both available?
2. What does the ad say about hours?
3. What does the ad say about benefits?
4. Why doesn't the ad give a phone number?

E.

> **Easy Work! Excellent Pay!**
> No experience.  Assemble
> products.  Call for info.
> 1-800-245-4847 ext. 252

1. How much experience do you need for this job?
2. What do you have to do?
3. What does ext. mean?
4. The ad says the work is easy and the pay is excellent.  Do you believe that?  Explain your answer.


5. Which of the five jobs in these ads would you apply for?  Why?

## *Homework*

Look at the Help-Wanted ads in a newspaper.  Circle in red two or three jobs that interest you.  Bring the ads into class.  To find the Help-Wanted ads, look at the index of the newspaper.  The index is usually on page 2.  Then look under Classified Ads.

# UNIT THREE WORD REVIEW

## I. SYNONYMS

Next to each sentence, write the word that has the same meaning or almost the same meaning as the part of the sentence in dark print.

| aims | average | shallow | foolish |
|------|---------|---------|---------|
| earn | at least | dull | quit |

1. _____ If we go by car, the trip will take **a minimum of** eight hours.

2. _____ The desk looks nice, but the drawers are **not deep**.

3. _____ On Friday we **stop** work an hour early.

4. _____ Heather **plans** to start her own business soon.

5. _____ The show was **not interesting**.

6. _____ I was **stupid** to listen to Nat. He didn't know what he was talking about.

7. _____ Michael Jackson isn't an **ordinary** singer. He's a superstar.

8. _____ Carpenters and plumbers **make** good money.

## II. SENTENCE COMPLETION

Complete the sentences with these words.

| hesitant | shouted | pool | shot |
|----------|---------|------|------|
| drag | bitter | dive | argue |

1. My sister and I often _____ about sports.

2. The detective _____ the man in the leg.

3. Juana and Diego are buying a _____ for their backyard.

4. A tree fell across the road.  It took three people to _____ it away and clear the road.

5. The Cold War between the United States and the Soviet Union was long and _____ .

6. I am _____ to accept a ride from someone I don't know.

7. It takes a lot of practice to learn to swim and _____ well.

8. When Adam saw that he was locked in the room, he _____ for help.

# III.  STORY COMPLETION

**Complete the story with these words.**

| | | | |
|---|---|---|---|
| lift | prefers | huge | spends |
| stream | hunting | deep | edge |

### *A Fisherman*

Howard and his cousin Neil often go _____, but Neil _____ to fish.  He _____ a lot of time fishing in a _____ a few miles from his house.  He stands at the _____ of the water and waits for the fish to bite.

Neil also enjoys fishing in the ocean where the water, of course, is _____ and the fish are larger.  One day when he was fishing in the ocean, Neil caught a _____ fish.  It was so heavy that he needed help to _____ it out of the water.  He's very proud of his big catch.

111

# UNIT FOUR

# Newcomers from Colombia

# C H A P T E R   T E N
# *A Struggle*

## PREVIEW QUESTIONS

**Discuss or think about these questions before reading the story.**

1. Why do most immigrants come to the United States?  Why did you come?
2. How did you feel when you first came?
3. How much English did you know?  Was that a big problem?  Explain your answer.

# A Struggle

Luis is from Medellín, the second largest city in Colombia. He loves Medellín, but he wasn't able to get a good job there. That's why he came to the United States ten years **ago.** He had a cousin in Philadelphia, and he shared an apartment with him for two years. Then he met and married Gloria, a pretty young girl from Medellín. They met at a dance in Philadelphia.

Life in the United States has been a **struggle** for Luis. The first year was especially difficult. He missed his family and friends back in Medellín. He had only a few relatives in Philadelphia and no friends  The weather was also a problem. He came to Philadelphia in January, and he **wasn't used to** the cold. It's never cold and it never snows in Medellín. During his second day in Philadelphia, there was a big **storm.** Twenty inches of snow fell in 24 hours. The snow was pretty, but Luis couldn't go anywhere for three days.

His biggest problem was to find a job. When he came to Philadelphia, he was only 20 and he didn't have many **skills.** But his cousin had a friend who worked at a **bakery** that needed help. Luis never **baked** before, but he learned by watching and working with another **baker.** He worked long hours baking bread, pies, and cake. It wasn't fun, but at least he had a job and could pay his expenses.

English was another problem. Luis didn't speak any English and understood very little. Fortunately, the other baker spoke Spanish. But Luis knew that English was important. Since he worked nights and slept in the morning, he studied English three afternoons a week at Philadelphia Community College on Market Street. In the beginning he was afraid of making mistakes, but his teacher was understanding and he learned quickly.

Luis worked at the bakery for five years, but he still wasn't making much money. He and a friend decided to quit and open their own bakery. "Of course it wasn't easy," he says. "We had to borrow money, hire workers, and rent a store. We didn't make any money for six months."

Now their business is doing very well. It's especially busy all day Saturday and on Sunday morning. Luis works hard and **accomplishes** a lot. He makes good money, saves some, and has a nice car. He also speaks English **quite** well and understands everything.

# I. COMPREHENSION QUESTIONS

**Answer these questions about the story.** *Use your judgment to answer questions with an asterisk. Work in pairs or small groups. The numbers in parentheses show which paragraph in the story has the answer.*

1. Why did Luis come to the United States? (1)
2. Why was the weather a problem for him? (2)
3. What happened his second day in Philadelphia? (2)
4. Why was it difficult for him to find a job? (3)
*5. Do you think people often get jobs with the help of a friend? Explain your answer.
6. How did Luis learn how to bake? (3)
7. How much English did he speak and understand when he came to the United States? (4)
8. What did he do to learn English? (4)
*9. Do you think he spoke much English outside of class? Do you? Explain your answers.
*10. Do you think fear of making mistakes often keeps people from speaking English?
11. What did Luis and his friend decide to do? (5)
12. When is their bakery especially busy? (6)

# II. WORD GUESSING

**Guess the meaning of the key words in these sentences.** *Use the context of the story and the sentences to guess. Circle your answers.*

1. Life in the United States has been *a* **struggle** for Luis.

   a. fun

   b. a mistake

   c. a waste of time

   d. hard work

2. He came to Philadelphia in January, and he **wasn't used to** the cold. It's never cold … in Medellín.

   a. wasn't afraid of

   b. wasn't familiar with

   c. wasn't happy about

   d. wasn't thinking about

3. Luis works hard and **accomplishes** a lot.

   a. talks

   b. helps others

   c. hurries

   d. does

# III. MINI-DICTIONARY — PART ONE

## Vocabulary Focus

1. **a·go** (ə-gō´)    *adjective:* before now; in the past
   "Nancy lived in New York for many years, but she moved to California six months **ago**."

2. **strug·gle** (strug´əl)    *noun:* hard work to get something; a fight
   *verb:* to work hard to get or do something
   "Learning English was a **struggle** for Mohammed."
   "Dave is **struggling** to support his family."

3. **be used to** (bē yo͞os to͞o *or* bē yo͞os´tə)    *idiom:* to be familiar with
   "Lauren **is used to** helping sick people; she's a nurse."

4. **storm** (stôrm)    *noun:* heavy rain or snow, often with a strong wind
   "A **storm** is coming.  We're going to get a lot of rain."

## Completing Sentences

**Complete the sentences with these words.**  *Use each word twice.  Where a word has different endings, both forms are given.*

is used to/am used to          ago          storm          struggle/struggling

1. Alan ate lunch an hour _____ .

2. Politics is a _____ for power.

3. I often work 12 hours a day.  I _____ working long hours.

4. Close the windows before you leave.  We may get a _____ .

5. Jason is very tired, but he wants to finish his homework. He's _____

   to stay awake.

6. If this _____ continues, we're staying home tonight.

7. Anna is a bus driver.  She _____ driving in bad weather.

8. Our new sofa came three days _____ .

## Creating Sentences

**Write an original sentence using these words.** *Work with a partner or on your own.*

1. (ago) _____

   _____

2. (struggle) _____

   _____

3. (be used to) _____

   _____

4. (storm) _____

   _____

# IV. MINI-DICTIONARY — PART TWO

5. **skill** (skil)   *noun:* ability to do something; ability to do something well
   "Reading and writing are basic **skills**."

6. a. **bake** (bāk)   *verb:* to cook in an oven
   "Jamie is **baking** cookies for the party."

   b. **bak·er** (bā´kər)   *noun:* a person who bakes
   "Mary Anne is a **baker**. She's taking the bread out of the ovens."

   c. **bak·er·y** (bāk´ə-rē *or* bāk´rē)   *noun:* a store that sells cakes, pies, bread, cookies, etc.
   "I'm going to the **bakery** to buy a birthday cake for my daughter."

7. **ac·com·plish** (ə-kom´plish)   *verb:* to do something; to do something well; to complete
   "We'll have to work hard to **accomplish** what we want to do."

8. **quite** (kwīt)   *adverb:* to some degree; very
   "This room is **quite** warm. I'm going to open the window."

## Completing Sentences

**Complete the sentences with these words.** *Use each word twice. Where a word has different endings, both forms are given.*

| accomplish/accomplished | skill | bake/baking | quite |
|---|---|---|---|

1. Typing is an important _____ for a secretary.

2. Stephanie is _____ tall.

3. Pete talks a lot, but he doesn't _____ much.

4. Jennifer is _____ fish for dinner.

5. Don is very good at fixing cars. This _____ got him a good job at the service station.

6. How long will it take to _____ the potatoes?

7. Tania is _____ intelligent. She should do well in school.

8. We _____ very little at yesterday's meeting.

## Creating Sentences

**Write an original sentence using these words.** *Work with a partner or on your own.*

5. (skill) _____

_____

6. (bake) _____

_____

7. (accomplish) _____

_____

8. (quite) _____

_____

# V.  STORY COMPLETION

**Discuss or think about these questions before completing the story that follows.**

1.  Do you think most couples eat out to celebrate their wedding anniversaries?
2.  How difficult is it for couples with young children to work full time?
3.  When do working couples with young children find time to shop and clean their homes?

**Complete the story with these words.**

| | | | |
|---|---|---|---|
| skill | storm | accomplish | baked |
| quite | are used to | struggle | ago |

### Vin and Marge

Vin and Marge got married six years _____ yesterday.  They were going to celebrate their anniversary by eating out, but there was a big _____ yesterday.  So much snow fell that they decided to stay home.  Vin cooked dinner, and Marge _____ a chocolate cake.  Vin isn't the best cook in the world, but the dinner tasted _____ good, and the cake was delicious.

Both Vin and Marge work full time, and they have two young children.  Working and taking care of two small children is often a _____.  It takes a lot of time, patience, and _____.

During the week, Vin and Marge have almost no free time, so they shop, clean the house, and visit their friends and relatives on the weekends.  They _____ a lot in two days.  It's not easy, but they _____ it by now.

# VI.  SHARING INFORMATION

**Discuss these questions and topics in pairs or small groups.**

1. How long **ago** did you start studying English?  How did you start?
2. People do things differently in different countries.  **Are** you **used to** the way people do things in the United States?  Are you used to the weather here?
3. Do you think that life is a **struggle** for everyone, including those who are rich?
4. There are many types of **storms**, for example, snowstorms, thunderstorms, and hurricanes. Describe a bad storm that you remember.
5. A **skill** is an ability to do something.  Cooking, driving, sewing, and typing are skills.  Name a skill that you have and one that you don't by completing these sentences.  I

   can _____ .  I can't _____ .

6. In the past, people **baked** more than they do today.  Why?
7. Name something you have **accomplished**, or that you are trying to accomplish.
8. Use the word **quite** to describe yourself or someone you know.  For example, "I'm quite thin."  "Frank is quite strong."

# VII.  WORD FAMILIES

**Complete the sentences with these words.**  *If necessary, add an ending to the word so it forms a correct sentence.*  (adj. = adjective and adv. = adverb)

1. **storm** (noun)               **stormy** (adj.)

   A. We can't go out in the boat today.  We're going to have a bad _____ .

   B. Look at those clouds!  It's going to be a _____ day.

2. **skill** (noun)          **skillful** (adj.)          **skillfully** (adv.)

   A. Ben is a _____ carpenter.

   B. A doctor needs a lot of _____ .

   C. The lawyer argued her case _____ .

3. **accomplish** (verb)               **accomplishment** (noun)

   A. Winning a gold medal in the Olympic Games is a great _____ .

   B. What do you hope to _____ today?

121

# VIII.  BUILDING NOUNS WITH -ION

The suffix **-ion** (**-tion, -ition, -ation, -sion**) is added to verbs to form a noun. For example, *protect + ion = protection; add + ition = addition.*

The suffix **-ion** usually means *the act of* or *the result of.* For example, *protection* means *the act or result of protecting; addition* means *the act or result of adding.*

| Verb | Noun | Verb | Noun |
|------|------|------|------|
| act | action | explore | exploration |
| add | addition | hesitate | hesitation |
| decide | decision | move | motion |
| discuss | discussion | prepare | preparation |
| educate | education | pronounce | pronunciation |
| examine | examination | protect | protection |
| explain | explanation | separate | separation |

**Circle the letter next to the word that *best* completes the sentence.**

1. The store owners asked the police for better _____ .
   - a. hesitation
   - b. protection
   - c. education
   - d. exploration

2. Our group had an interesting _____ about marriage.
   - a. action
   - b. addition
   - c. pronunciation
   - d. discussion

3. The _____ of the ship made me sick.
   - a. motion
   - b. preparation
   - c. explanation
   - d. separation

4. A good _____ will help you get a job.
   - a. protection
   - b. hesitation
   - c. education
   - d. addition

5. Your _____ of English is much better now.
    a. separation             c. decision
    b. addition               d. pronunciation

6. Our history _____ was long and difficult, but I think I did well.
    a. examination         c. hesitation
    b. protection            d. motion

7. It was very cold this morning, but my car started without _____ .
    a. exploration          c. hesitation
    b. protection            d. discussion

8. We have to do more than just talk about the problem. We must take

   _____ .
    a. education            c. examination
    b. action                d. addition

# C H A P T E R   E L E V E N
# *A Dream*

## PREVIEW QUESTIONS

**Discuss or think about these questions before reading the story.**

1. Are you happy with the apartment you rent?  Or the house you rent or own?
2. How much does it cost to rent a two-bedroom apartment in good condition?
3. How much does it cost to buy a house in a nice neighborhood in the city where you live?

# A Dream

Luis and his wife Gloria live in a nice apartment, but it isn't big **enough**. The kitchen and the living room are small. There are only two bedrooms, and they need three. They have two sons, Carlos and Diego, and a daughter, Maria, and they want her to have her own room. She's seven and the boys are four and two. They also want to have a yard for the children to play in.

Their **dream** is to buy a house, and they have already looked at some that are for sale. One of them was beautiful and had a modern kitchen, central air conditioning, and a big yard, but it was terribly expensive. Luis and Gloria don't have enough money to buy it. The bakery is their only income, and it isn't doing well enough to allow them to buy an expensive house. That's why they're **searching** for one that doesn't cost a lot, and, of course, that's not easy to find.

Yesterday they looked at four houses, and three of them were great. They didn't need painting and were in good repair, and one of them had a pool. But it was the same story. They couldn't afford the houses they liked, and they didn't like the house they could afford.

The affordable one was old and had **cracks** in the walls. The owner didn't take care of it. Now he has to move to Ohio to take a new job, and he's in a hurry to sell. The house needs painting and many **repairs**, but has one **advantage** — it costs $50,000 to $70,000 less than the other three houses.

Last night Luis and Gloria talked about the house for two hours. "I know we won't find anything that costs less, and I want to move as soon as I can," said Luis. "And I'm tired of looking at houses we can't afford," Gloria added. **So** they decided to buy the old house and repair it.

The house will **require** a lot of work, but it's in a nice neighborhood and the back yard is big. It'll look beautiful when they're finished with it. Luis and Gloria are good at painting, and some of their friends will help with the repairs. The children will be happy to have their own house where they can make all the noise they want, and Maria will be especially happy to have her own room. Tomorrow Luis and Gloria are going to a bank to ask for a loan.

# I. COMPREHENSION QUESTIONS

## *True or False*

**If the sentence is true, write T.  If it's false, write F and change it to a true statement.**

_____ 1. Luis and Gloria have a large apartment.

_____

_____ 2. They want Maria to have her own room.

_____

_____ 3. They have already looked at some houses, and one was very nice.

_____

_____ 4. They can easily find a house they can afford.

_____

_____ 5. They didn't like any of the houses they looked at yesterday.

_____

_____ 6. The house they can afford needs painting and many repairs.

_____

_____ 7. Luis wants to move, but he's in no hurry.

_____

_____ 8. Luis and Gloria plan to do a lot of their own work on the house.

_____

## What Do You Think?

**Use your experience, judgment, and the story to answer these questions.** *The story alone won't answer them.*

1. The cost of a house depends on many things, for example, its location. What else does its cost depend on?

2. Luis and Gloria are going to paint and repair their home with the help of some friends. Will that save them a lot of money? Explain your answer.

3. Why can't the children make all the noise they want in their apartment?

4. What questions will they ask Luis and Gloria at the bank?

# II.   WORD GUESSING

**Guess the meaning of the key words in these sentences.** *Use the context of the story and the sentences to guess. Circle your answers.*

1. *Their* **dream** *is to* buy a house, and they have already looked at some that are for sale.

   a. they think it's easy to     c. they know they can

   b. they want very much to     d. they know they can't

2. That's why Luis and Gloria are **searching** *for* a house that doesn't cost a lot, and, of course, that's not easy to find.

   a. buying     c. looking for

   b. hoping for     d. thinking of

3. **So** Luis and Gloria decided to buy the old house and repair it.

   a. that's why     c. later

   b. but     d. however

# III.   MINI-DICTIONARY — PART ONE

## Vocabulary Focus

1. **e·nough** (i-nuf´)     *adjective:* as much or as many as needed; sufficient

                           *adverb:* to the amount or degree needed

   "Do we have **enough** time to stop and visit our friends?"

   "My car is big **enough***** for five people."

   *****When **enough** is used as an adverb, it is placed after the adjective or adverb it goes with.

127

2. **dream** (drēm)   *noun:*  A. images the mind sees in sleep

                                              B. something one wants, but that is difficult or impossible to get

                     *verb:*  to have a dream

"I went to sleep and had a **dream** that I was the president of the United States."

"Last night Wayne **dreamt** he won a million dollars in the lottery."

The past of **dream** is **dreamed** or **dreamt**.

3. **search** (sûrch)   *verb:*  to look for or through something carefully

                     *noun:*  the act of looking for or through something carefully

"Nick is **searching** everywhere for his ring."

"In 1849 many people rushed to California in **search** of gold."

4. **crack** (krak)   *noun:*  a small break or separation in a wall, cup, etc.

                   *verb:*  to cause a small separation in a cup, dish, etc.

"There's a **crack** in the mirror."

"The water was so hot that it **cracked** a dish."

## *Completing Sentences*

**Complete the sentences with these words.** *Use each word twice. Where a word has different endings, both forms are given.*

| search/searching | enough | crack/cracked | dream/dreamt |
|---|---|---|---|

1. The engineers are checking the _____ in the bridge.

2. Grace is _____ for a job.

3. I don't know what it means, but I _____ about you last night.

4. That's _____ spaghetti. I can't eat any more.

5. After a long _____, my husband found his keys.

6. I dropped the glass and it _____.

7. Gene isn't fast _____ to win the race.

8. Manuela's _____ is to be a doctor.

## Creating Sentences

**Write an original sentence using these words.** *Work with a partner or on your own.*

1. (enough) _____

2. (dream) _____

3. (search) _____

4. (crack) _____

# IV.  MINI-DICTIONARY — PART TWO

## Vocabulary Focus

5. **re·pair** (ri-pâr´)  *verb:* to put in good condition again; to fix

     *noun:* the act of putting in good condition again

   "They're going to **repair** the road in the spring.  It's in poor condition."

   "I have to bring my car to the service station for **repairs**."  (**Repair** is often used in the plural.)

6. **ad·van·tage** (ad-van´tij)  *noun:* anything that helps a person or thing do or be better

   "A good education is a big **advantage** in life."

7. **so** (sō)  *adverb:* that is why; for that reason*

   "We were hungry, **so** we stopped to eat."

   ***So** has other meanings.  It often means *very*.  "Everyone likes Tina.  She's so nice."

8. **re·quire** (ri-kwīr´)  *verb:* A. to need

     B. to say something is necessary; to order

   "Dogs are great pets, but they **require** a lot of care."

## Completing Sentences

**Complete the sentences with these words.** *Use each word twice.  Where a word has different endings, both forms are given.*

| repair/repairs | so | advantage/advantages | require/requires |
|---|---|---|---|

1. The restaurant we're going to _____ men to wear jackets.

2. Jan had a toothache, _____ he went to the dentist.

3. The elevator isn't working.  I hope they _____ it soon.

4. The _____ of leaving early is that traffic will be light.

5. Most babies _____ ten or eleven hours of sleep a night.

6. Our TV is new.  It shouldn't need any _____ .

7. Money isn't everything, but it has its _____ .

8. The suit was very expensive, _____ I didn't buy it.

## *Creating Sentences*

**Write an original sentence using these words.**  *Work with a partner or on your own.*

5. (repair) _____

6. (advantage) _____

7. (so) _____

8. (require) _____

# V.  STORY COMPLETION

**Discuss or think about these questions before completing the story that follows.**

1. Do you dream much?  Can you remember a dream you had recently?
2. A dream in which something very bad happens is called a nightmare.  Do you ever have nightmares?
3. Do you believe in dreams — do you think that what you see in a dream is likely to happen in real life?

### Complete the story with these words.

| so | enough | searching | advantages |
|---|---|---|---|
| repair | dreamed | require | cracks |

## The Old School Bus

Jack is a mechanic who works for a public school system in Pennsylvania. Part of his job is to check the school buses and keep them in good condition. Last night he _____ that the old school bus at the high school was missing and that everyone was _____ for it. One of the high school students had taken it and had a terrible accident.

This morning the first thing Jack did was to check the old bus. The motor didn't sound right, it needed new brakes, and a window and some of the seats had _____ in them. Jack felt the bus wasn't safe _____ for the students. _____ he's writing a report for the high school principal and the board of education.

The report says it's possible to _____ the bus, but it'll _____ a lot of work, and that'll be expensive. It would be better to buy a new one.

There are many _____ to a new bus. It'll be bigger, cleaner, and much safer. It'll be less expensive to maintain. As soon as he finishes the report, Jack is going to give it to Mrs. Johnson, the high school principal.

# VI. SHARING INFORMATION

**Discuss these questions and topics in pairs or small groups.**

1. Do you have **enough** space in the apartment or house in which you live? For example, are the kitchen and the closets big enough?

2. We all have **dreams**, hopes for the future. Complete this sentence: My dream is to

_____ .

3. When we lose something that is valuable, we **search** for it. Name something you lost and searched for. Did you find it?

4. We see **cracks** in many things, for example, windows. Name some other things in which we often see cracks.

5. When a person is good at making small **repairs**, we say that person is handy, good with his or her hands. Are you handy?

6. Many people leave their family, friends, and country to live in the United States or Canada. What are some of the **advantages** of living in the United States or Canada? What are some **disadvantages**?

7. Complete this sentence: Ernie has a headache and fever, so he _____

   _____ .

8. Our bodies **require** rest. Name four other things our bodies require.

   1. _____    2. _____

   3. _____    4. _____

# VII. WORD FAMILIES

**Complete the sentences with these words.** *If necessary, add an ending to the word so it forms a correct sentence.* (adj. = adjective and adv. = adverb)

1. **advantage** (noun)                **advantageous** (adj.)
   **take advantage of** (idiom)       **disadvantage** (noun)

   A. Roger is going to college in September. He doesn't know anything about

   computers. That's a (an) _____ .

   B. Our army was in a (an) _____ position when the enemy attacked.

   C. We should _____ this nice weather and go for a walk.

   D. Caroline is very tall. That's a (an) _____ when she plays basketball.

2. **require** (verb)                **requirement** (noun)

   A. That's a bad cut! It's going to _____ stitches.

   B. A high school education is a _____ for many jobs.

# VIII. BUILDING WORDS WITH **DIS-**

The prefix **dis-** is placed before nouns, adjectives, and verbs to form a new word. For example, *dis + honest = dishonest; dis + advantage = disadvantage.*

The prefix **dis-** means *not* or *the opposite of.* For example, *dishonest* means *not honest; disadvantage* is *the opposite of advantage.*

132

| Original Word | New Word | Original Word | New Word |
|---|---|---|---|
| advantage | disadvantage | order | disorder |
| appear | disappear | please | displease |
| continue | discontinue | repair | disrepair |
| courage | discourage | respect | disrespect |
| honest | dishonest | satisfied | dissatisfied |
| like | dislike | trust | distrust |
| obey | disobey | | |

**Circle the letter next to the word that *best* completes the sentence.**

1. If we don't pay our phone bill soon, they'll _____ our service.
   - a. disobey
   - b. discourage
   - c. discontinue
   - d. dislike

2. Courtney doesn't like her teacher, but she never shows any _____.
   - a. disrespect
   - b. disrepair
   - c. disadvantage
   - d. disorder

3. We don't trust George. We think he's _____.
   - a. discouraged
   - b. dishonest
   - c. dissatisfied
   - d. displeased

4. What's the _____ of living in a big city?
   - a. disadvantage
   - b. disrepair
   - c. dislike
   - d. disorder

5. I'm going to another dentist. I _____ the one I have.
   - a. discourage
   - b. disobey
   - c. displease
   - d. dislike

6. If there is any more _____ at this party, I'm calling the police.
   - a. disrespect
   - b. disrepair
   - c. disorder
   - d. distrust

7. My wallet _____. I can't find it anywhere.
   - a. disobeyed
   - b. discontinued
   - c. disliked
   - d. disappeared

8. After many years of _____, it's going to be difficult to fix the building.
   - a. disadvantages
   - b. disrepair
   - c. distrust
   - d. disrespect

# CHAPTER TWELVE
## *A Visit*

## PREVIEW QUESTIONS

**Discuss or think about these questions before reading the story.**

1. Do you visit friends or relatives often?  How often?
2. Do you go to sleep easily?
3. Did you ever fall asleep when visiting friends?

# A Visit

Saturday is always Luis' busiest day, but last Saturday was busier than most. One of his bakers was sick, and that meant more work for Luis. When he came home from work, he was **weary**. He wanted to stay home, watch a little TV, and go to bed early, but Gloria wanted to visit some of their friends from Medellín, Colombia. She had told their friends they were coming and the friends were expecting them, so they couldn't stay home.

When Gloria and Luis arrived at their friends' house, he knew it was going to be difficult not to **fall asleep**. He falls asleep easily. Every night he watches the 10:00 news, and every night he's asleep before the news is over. So he was happy when his friend offered him some coffee. "I hope it's Colombian," he joked. "Of course it is, that's the only kind we serve," his friend replied with a smile. Luis drank two cups of black coffee, but he could **hardly** keep his eyes open.

Luis and Gloria were sitting in the living room, and he was okay **while** their friends were showing them photos. But when everyone started talking about the good old days in Medellín, he fell asleep. Gloria was next to him on the sofa. She **pinched** his arm, but it didn't help. She pinched him again. This time he **woke up**.

Luis drank another cup of coffee, and his friend opened a window for him. Luis knew Gloria wasn't happy about his falling asleep. He tried hard to stay awake. He was fine for a **while**, but then he fell asleep again and began to snore.* When Luis snores, he makes a lot of noise.

Gloria was **ashamed**. She was ashamed of Luis' snoring and she was angry at him. Their friends came to the United States three months ago, and this was the first time they had visited them. However, his snoring didn't **disturb** them. They smiled and told Gloria to let him sleep. They know how hard he works.

On the the way home, Gloria and Luis had a little argument. "I think you should try harder to stay awake when we're visiting friends," she remarked. "And I think you should be smart enough not to visit friends on Saturday nights," he replied. "You know how tired I am after work on Saturday." Then he said he was sorry that he fell asleep and snored. She gave him a kiss and everything was okay.

---

*Snore means *to make noise through one's nose and mouth while sleeping.*

# I. COMPREHENSION QUESTIONS

**Answer these questions about the story.** *Use your judgment to answer questions with an asterisk. Work in pairs or small groups. The numbers in parentheses show which paragraph in the story has the answer.*

1. Why was last Saturday busier than most for Luis? (1)
2. What did he want to do when he came home from work? (1)
*3. Do you think Gloria should have called their friends and said they couldn't visit them that night because Luis was too tired?
4. What happens to Luis when he watches the 10:00 news? (2)
*5. Why does coffee keep people awake? Does it keep you awake?
6. When did Luis fall asleep? (3)
7. What did Gloria do when he fell asleep? (3)
8. What did he do after he fell asleep again? (4)
9. How did Luis' snoring make Gloria feel? (5)
10. How did their friends feel about his snoring? (5)
*11. Do you think this was the first time Luis fell asleep while visiting friends? Or do you think it happened before? Explain your answer.
12. What did Luis say that ended their argument? (6)

# II. WORD GUESSING

**Guess the meaning of the key words in these sentences.** *Use the context of the story and the sentences to guess. Circle your answers.*

1. When Luis came home from work, he was **weary**.

   a. hungry
   b. tired
   c. happy
   d. thirsty

2. Gloria *was* **ashamed**. She was ashamed of Luis' snoring.

   a. was sad
   b. was angry
   c. was quiet
   d. felt bad

3. However, the snoring didn't **disturb** *their friends*.

   a. make them laugh
   b. make them say anything
   c. make them unhappy
   d. make them think badly of him

# III. MINI-DICTIONARY — PART ONE

## Vocabulary Focus

1. **wear·y** (wir´ē)   *adjective:* very tired
   "The basketball team has been practicing for three hours, and the players are **weary**."

2. **fall a·sleep** (fôl ə-slēp´)   *idiom:* to begin to sleep
   "Leo went to bed and immediately **fell asleep**. He was tired."
   The past of **fall** is **fell**.

3. **hard·ly** (härd´lē)   *adverb:* only a little; with difficulty
   "Speak louder, please. We can **hardly** hear you."

4. **while** (wīl *or* hwīl)   *conjunction:* during the time that
   *noun:* an indefinite period of time, usually short
   "I read a magazine **while** I was waiting for the dentist."
   "Dinner will be ready in a little **while** ."

## Completing Sentences

**Complete the sentences with these words.** *Use each word twice. Where a word has different endings, both forms are given.*

**hardly**          **weary**          **while**          **falls asleep/fell asleep**

1. _____ you were watching TV, I was doing the dishes.

2. It's _____ raining now. I'm not going to wear a raincoat.

3. When Gary comes home from work, he sits down in his favorite chair and

   _____ .

4. The battle lasted for three days, and the soldiers are _____ .

5. The meeting was long and the room was hot. That's why I _____ .

6. Take a break and rest a _____ .

7. My neighbor wanted to borrow my car, but I didn't let him. I _____ know him.

8. By the end of the day we were _____ .

## Creating Sentences

**Write an original sentence using these words.** *Work with a partner or on your own.*

1. (weary) _____

_____

2. (fall asleep) _____

_____

3. (hardly) _____

_____

4. (while) _____

_____

# IV.  MINI-DICTIONARY — PART TWO

## Vocabulary Focus

5. **pinch** (pinch)   *verb:* to press hard between the thumb and another finger

  *noun:* A. the act of pinching

  B. a small amount

"The baby likes to **pinch** his mother's neck and face."

"That **pinch** hurt. Don't pinch me again!"

6. **wake up** (wāk up)   *verb:* A. to stop sleeping

  B. to cause a person to stop sleeping

"The alarm clock **woke up** Fred." *Or* "The alarm clock **woke** Fred **up**."*

The past of **wake up** is **woke up**.

*A noun object of *wake up* may be placed before or after *up*. A pronoun object must be placed between *wake* and *up*. "The alarm clock **woke** him **up**."

7. a. **shame** (shām)  *noun:* an unpleasant feeling that comes from doing something that we think is wrong or foolish

   b. **a·shamed** (ə-shāmd´)  *adjective:* feeling shame

      "I'm **ashamed** of getting drunk at the party."

8. **dis·turb** (dis-tûrb´)  *verb:* to take away a person's peace or quiet

   "Please turn down the music. I'm trying to study and it's **disturbing** me."

## Completing Sentences

**Complete the sentences with these words.** *Use each word twice. Where a word has different endings, both forms are given.*

wake up/woke up       ashamed       disturb/disturbing       pinch/pinched

1. You should be ————————— of taking that radio from the store.

2. Bobby didn't like it when I ————————— his side.

3. ————————— ! It's late! You have to go to work!

4. Nicole is writing an important letter. Don't ————————— her!

5. Jonathan added a ————————— of salt to the mashed potatoes.

6. Karen felt ————————— that she forgot her father's birthday.

7. The company's decision to close the factory is ————————— .

8. Tim ————————— at 6:00 A.M.

## Creating Sentences

**Write an original sentence using these words.** *Work with a partner or on your own.*

5. (pinch) ————————————————————————

   ————————————————————————————

6. (wake up) ———————————————————————

   ————————————————————————————

7. (ashamed) ———————————————————————

   ————————————————————————————

8. (disturb) _____

## V. STORY COMPLETION

**Discuss or think about these questions before completing the story that follows.**

1. How many of your classes are dull?  All of them?  Most?  Some?  One?  None?
2. Did (do) you ever fall asleep in class?  If so, why?
3. If a student frequently falls asleep in class, do you think the teacher will give the student a lower mark?  Explain your answer.

**Complete the story with these words.**

| disturbs | pinch | weary | falls asleep |
|---|---|---|---|
| hardly | while | wakes | ashamed |

### A Dull Teacher

Cindy works during the day and goes to college at night.  Most of her classes are interesting, but her English teacher is dull.  He never changes his tone of voice and the students call him "Mr. Monotone."

At the beginning of class, Cindy is fine, but after a _____ she feels tired, and sometimes she _____.  The teacher doesn't say anything, but he sees her sleeping and it really _____ him.  He tries to make his class interesting, but it never is.

Cindy isn't _____ of going to sleep in class, but she is afraid of getting a poor mark.  She wants at least a B.  So she has asked a friend who sits behind her to _____ her when she goes to sleep.  This _____ her up, but Cindy is still so _____ that she can _____ stay awake.

# VI.  SHARING INFORMATION

**Discuss these questions and topics in pairs or small groups.**

1. Long physical or mental activity often makes us **weary**.  Complete this sentence:

   After I _____ for a long time, I often feel weary.

2. Do you ever **fall asleep** while watching TV?  Often?  Does coffee or tea keep you from falling asleep?

3. Think of something you can do only with difficulty, something you can do, but almost can't.  For example, "I can **hardly** swim."  Then complete this sentence:  I can

   hardly _____ .

4. A **while** is an indefinite period of time, usually a short period, but sometimes long.  Name something that you haven't done in a long while.  Name someone you haven't seen in a long while.

5. Sometimes people give a child a little **pinch** on the cheek to express their affection.  Do you think children like this?  Did you when you were a child?

6. What time do you usually **wake up** in the morning?  Who or what wakes you up?

7. Sometimes we feel **ashamed** when we shouldn't, but there are times when people should feel ashamed.  Complete this sentence:  I think people should feel ashamed

   when they _____ .

8. Give an example of something or somebody that **disturbs** you.

# VII.  WORD FAMILIES

**Complete the sentences with these words.** *If necessary, add an ending to the word so it forms a correct sentence.*  (adj. = adjective and adv. = adverb)

1. **weary** (adj.)                    **weariness** (noun)

   A. Sleep is the best cure for _____ .

   B. I'm often _____ on Friday afternoon.

2. **fall asleep** (idiom)              **asleep** (adj.)

   A. After I go to bed, it's a while before I _____ .

   B. The children are in bed, but they aren't _____ .  I hear them

   talking.

141

3. **wake up** (idiom)                    **awake** (adj.)

   A. It's 1:00 in the morning, but Phil is still _____ . He's reading.

   B. Shh.  Talk quietly.  Don't _____ the baby.

4. **disturb** (verb)                    **disturbance** (noun)

   A. It _____ me when people smoke in my house, but I don't like to

   say anything.

   B. There was a _____ at the dance, but it wasn't serious.

# VIII.  BUILDING NOUNS WITH -ANCE OR -ENCE

The suffix **-ance** or **-ence** is added to verbs and adjectives to form a noun.  For example, *accept + ance = acceptance; clear + ance = clearance.*  Words that already end in *ant* or *ent* drop the final *t* and add only *ce*.  For example, *intelligent* drops its final *t* and adds *ce* to form *intelligence.*

When *ance* or *ence* is added to a verb, it means *the act of* or *the result of.*  For example, *acceptance* means *the act of accepting* or *the result of accepting.*

When *ance* or *ence* is added to an adjective, it means *the quality of being.*  For example, *intelligence* means *the quality of being intelligent.*

| Verb or Adjective | Noun |
| --- | --- |
| accept | acceptance |
| appear | appearance |
| assist | assistance |
| clear | clearance |
| different | difference |
| disturb | disturbance |
| enter | entrance |
| excellent | excellence |
| important | importance |
| independent | independence |
| intelligent | intelligence |
| obedient | obedience |
| silent | silence |

142

**Circle the letter next to the word that *best* completes the sentence.**

1. The United States celebrates its _____ on July 4th.
   - a. importance
   - b. independence
   - c. acceptance
   - d. difference

2. We need a lawyer with a lot of skill and _____.
   - a. clearance
   - b. silence
   - c. obedience
   - d. intelligence

3. Everyone knows the _____ of good health.
   - a. importance
   - b. difference
   - c. entrance
   - d. acceptance

4. Glenda is waiting for a letter of _____ from college.
   - a. appearance
   - b. excellence
   - c. acceptance
   - d. independence

5. There's a big _____ between the weather in New York and in Florida.
   - a. disturbance
   - b. clearance
   - c. assistance
   - d. difference

6. They're having a (an) _____ sale at the furniture store.
   - a. acceptance
   - b. entrance
   - c. clearance
   - d. appearance

7. Thanks a lot for your _____ at the party.
   - a. assistance
   - b. difference
   - c. obedience
   - d. importance

8. In the army, _____ is very important. You must follow orders.
   - a. appearance
   - b. obedience
   - c. independence
   - d. clearance

# IX. LOOKING FOR AN APARTMENT AND A HOUSE

Luis and Gloria rented an apartment after they got married. Some years later they bought a house. In looking for an apartment and later for a house, they read many newspaper ads like the ones that follow. Ads A and B are rentals. C, D, and E are houses for sale.

| Abbreviation | Meaning |
|---|---|
| 1. apt. | apartment |
| 2. lg. or lrg. | large |
| 3. DR | dining room |
| 4. LR | living room |
| 5. BR | bedroom |
| 6. bth. or bathrm. | bathroom |
| 7. mod. kit. | modern kitchen |
| 8. fin. bsmnt. | finished basement |
| 9. FP or fplc. | fireplace |
| 10. w/w crptg. | wall to wall carpeting |
| 11. gar. | garage |
| 12. yrd. | yard |
| 13. H/HW incl. | heat/hot water included |
| 14. w/ | with |
| 15. betwn. | between |
| 16. move in cond. | move in condition |
| 17. avail. immed. | available immediately |
| 18. schls. | schools |
| 19. transp. | transportation |
| 20. shpg. | shopping |

**A.**

> beautiful 2 BR apt., mod.
> kit., bath., LR, H/HW incl.
> avail. immed., $600/mo.
> call 201-338-1872

1. How many bedrooms does this apartment have?
2. What does the ad say about the kitchen?
3. Do you have to pay extra for heat and hot water?
4. When will you be able to rent the apartment?
5. How much rent will you have to pay?

**B.**

> 1 & 2 BR apts. avail., new
> kit. and bth., new w/w crptg.,
> h/hw incl., near transp.,
> no pets, call betwn. 9 am &
> 9 pm, ask for Maria.
> 201-678-4591

1. What does the ad say about the kitchens and bathrooms?
2. What type of carpeting do the apartments have?
3. Can you keep a dog in these apartments?
4. Why are these apartments good for someone who doesn't own a car?
5. How can you find out how much the apartments rent for?

**C.**

> 4 lg. BRs, DR, 2 bths.,
> mod. kit., 2 car gar.,
> near schls. & shpg.,
> $150,000.
> 908-276-4242

1. What does the ad say about the bedrooms in this house?
2. How many bathrooms does it have?
3. What's special about the garage?
4. What's good about the location of the house?
5. How much does it cost?

**D.**

> LR w/fplc., DR, mod.
> eat in kit., 3 BRs, 1 1/2
> bths., fin. bsmnt., lge.
> yard.  Realtor.
> 201-692-2303

1. What's special about the living room in this house?
2. What does the ad say about the kitchen?
3. How many bathrooms are there?
4. What kind of basement does the house have?
5. How does the ad describe the yard?

**E.**

> By owner: low taxes,
> lrg. LR, 2 BRs, eat in kit.,
> full sized bsmnt., move in
> cond., 2 car driveway,
> fenced in yrd. $130,000.
> 202-784-9269

1. Why do you think the owner is selling the house without a real estate agent?
2. What type of kitchen does the house have?
3. What condition is the house in?
4. Does the house have a garage?  Explain your answer.
5. What does the ad say about the yard?

Which of the houses (C, D, or E) do you like best?

## *Homework*

Look at the apartments for rent and houses for sale in the classified section of a newspaper.  Circle in red an apartment for rent and a house for sale, and bring the ads into class.

# UNIT FOUR WORD REVIEW

## I.   SYNONYMS

Next to each sentence, write the word that has the same meaning or almost the same meaning as the part of the sentence in dark print.

baking                    storm                    required                    weary

accomplish                while                    searching                   so

1. _____   Tony has two jobs.  When he finishes the second, he's **tired**.

2. _____   We're going to get a **lot of wind and rain** tonight.

3. _____   Yoko is **looking** for the money she lost.

4. _____   The bank **needed** more information before they would give me a loan.

5. _____   It was cloudy and cool on Saturday.  **That's why** we didn't go to the beach.

6. _____   Steve is **cooking** the beans **in the oven**.

7. _____   It takes a **little time** for the car to warm up.

8. _____   Beth and I hope to **do** a lot tomorrow.

# II. SENTENCE COMPLETION

### Complete the sentences with these words.

| | | | |
|---|---|---|---|
| skill | disturbs | wake up | crack |
| fell asleep | advantage | ashamed | pinched |

1. I have to _____ the children soon, or they'll be late for school.

2. Both Greg and Alexi are good carpenters, but Greg has more experience and

   _____ .

3. I _____ myself to keep from laughing at my friend. She was wearing

   a funny hat.

4. Marilyn speaks French well; that will give her a (an) _____ when she

   visits Paris.

5. Marissa should be _____ of lying to her parents.

6. There is a _____ in the lamp. It fell on the floor.

7. It _____ Jenny when her neighbors have noisy parties.

8. Hank _____ while driving, and his car went off the road.

   Fortunately, it didn't hit anything.

# III.  STORY COMPLETION

**Complete the story with these words.**

| | | | | |
|---|---|---|---|---|
| repairing | while | enough | dream | ago |
| quite | hardly | struggle | was used to | |

### A Hard Worker

Andrew was born thirty years _____ in eastern Poland.  He was the oldest of three children, and his father was a coal miner.  His father worked hard, but was paid very little.  The family was _____ poor.

Andrew's _____ was to live in the United States.  He could _____ speak English, but he was very good at _____ cars and he _____ hard work.

Andrew was very happy when he got his visa and left for the United States.  However, finding a job in the United States was a _____ . The biggest problem was that he didn't know _____ English.  He worked in a factory _____ looking for a job as an auto mechanic.  After a few months, he got a job as a mechanic at a service station, and he's doing very well now.

# UNIT FIVE

# *Newcomers from Italy*

# CHAPTER THIRTEEN
# *Soccer Fans*

? ? ? ? ? ? ? ? ? ? ? ? ? ? ? ? ? ? ? ? ? ? ? ?

# PREVIEW QUESTIONS

**Discuss or think about these questions before reading the story.**

1. Do you like soccer?*  Is it your favorite sport?
2. Do you play soccer?  Do you watch it on TV?
3. Name some countries in which it's a very popular sport.
4. Why is it so popular in so many countries?

   *In many countries soccer is called *futbol*.  American football is a very different game.

# Soccer Fans

Mario lives in Chicago, and he comes from Italy. He's a barber, and he's married and has two children, Sal and Marie. His wife, Connie, is also Italian, but she was born in the United States. She stays home and takes care of the children, but she plans to go to work when the children are older. She's more modern than Mario.

Mario and Connie are big soccer **fans.** But when Mario came to the United States eight years ago, he didn't know that soccer was a popular sport here. The only American sports that he heard a lot about were basketball, baseball, and football. He was **amazed** to learn that there were many soccer teams in the United States.

One Sunday afternoon, he was taking a walk and **discovered** two teams playing soccer in a park near his house. He watched the game. Both teams had excellent players, and the game was **exciting.** When it was over, he talked to some of the players. They were from Italy, Spain, and Latin America. One of the teams needed another player, and they asked Mario to **join** them. He was happy to do so. Seven years later he's still playing on the team, and he's one of their best players.

His son Sal is also learning how to play soccer, and he goes to all of his dad's games. Mario practices with him and shows him how to kick and pass the ball. He's only six years old, but he's fast and can kick and pass well. His ability to play soccer is amazing. "Like father, like son," their friends say. And Sal says, "I can't wait until I'm old enough to play on the team at my school."

Last week Mario, Connie, and their two kids drove all the way from Chicago to New Jersey to visit Connie's cousins. It took them two days. She hadn't seen her cousins for five years, but the biggest reason for the trip was that her youngest cousin was getting married. She didn't want to miss the big wedding and the family reunion.

Her cousins are also crazy about soccer. One night her cousin Lou was playing. It was the final game of the season, and the entire family went to the game. There was a large **crowd.** Mario and Connie **cheered** when Lou's team played well. The **score** was 2 to 2 at half time. It was exciting. No one **scored** in the third quarter, and then with only 60 seconds left, Lou scored, and his team won 3 to 2. After the game they went to have pizza and to celebrate.

# I. COMPREHENSION QUESTIONS

**Answer these questions about the story.** *Use your judgment to answer questions with an asterisk. Work in pairs or small groups. The numbers in parentheses show which paragraph in the story has the answer.*

1. What does Mario do? And Connie? (1)
*2. Why do you think she's more modern than Mario?
3. What were the only American sports that he heard a lot about? (2)
*4. Why isn't soccer more popular in the United States?
5. What did Mario discover? (3)
6. What did he do after the game? (3)
*7. Do you think he's proud of Sal? Explain your answer.
8. Why doesn't Sal play soccer for his school team? (4)
9. What did Mario, Connie, and the kids do last week? (5)
10. What was the biggest reason for their trip? (5)
11. What did they do when Lou's team played well? (6)
12. What did Lou do with 60 seconds left? (6)

# II. WORD GUESSING

**Guess the meaning of the key words in these sentences.** *Use the context of the story and the sentences to guess. Circle your answers.*

1. Mario and Connie *are big soccer* **fans.**

   a. play a lot of soccer     c. coach a soccer team
   b. watch soccer on TV     d. are very interested in soccer

2. Mario was **amazed** to learn that there were many soccer teams in the United States.

   a. glad     c. quick
   b. surprised     d. slow

3. Both teams had excellent players and the game was **exciting.**

   a. long     c. very interesting
   b. close     d. dull

# III. MINI-DICTIONARY — PART ONE

## Vocabulary Focus

1. **fan** (fan)    *noun:* someone who has a great interest in a sport or a famous person*

   "Dick is a big basketball **fan**. He goes to a lot of games and watches them on TV."

   *A **fan** is also *an instrument to make air move so it will feel cool.* "In the summer we put a **fan** in our living room."

2. **a·maze** (ə-māze´)    *verb:* to surprise very much

   "Victor **amazed** his teacher by getting 100 on his test."

3. **dis·cov·er** (dis-kuv´ər)    *verb:* to find or come to know something not known before

   "Many people rushed to California in 1849 after someone **discovered** gold."

4. **ex·cit·ing** (ik-sī´ting)    *adjective:* causing strong feelings

   "The book was so **exciting** that I couldn't put it down."

## Completing Sentences

**Complete the sentences with these words.** *Use each word twice. Where a word has different endings, both forms are given.*

discover/discovered        fan        exciting        amazes/amazed

1. Everyone liked the movie. It was _____ .

2. My daughter is a tennis _____.

3. The astronauts _____ the world when they landed on the moon.

4. I was angry when I _____ that someone took my money.

5. Carol is a _____ of Bruce Springsteen. She loves to hear him sing.

6. Our trip to Africa was _____ .

7. Doctors are trying to _____ a cure for cancer.

8. The little boy plays the piano so well. He _____ me.

## Creating Sentences

**Write an original sentence using these words.** *Work with a partner or on your own.*

1. (fan) _____

_____

2. (amaze) _____

_____

3. (discover) _____

_____

4. (exciting) _____

_____

# IV.  MINI-DICTIONARY — PART TWO

## Vocabulary Focus

5. **join** (join)     *verb:* A. to become a member of a group
                              B. to unite
   "Lisa is going to **join** the army next week."

6. **crowd** (kroud)     *noun:* many people in one place
   "The police are having trouble controlling the **crowd**."

7. **cheer** (chēr)     *verb:* to shout or clap for a team or person
                              *noun:* shouting and clapping for a team or person
   "The president is going by in his limousine and everyone is **cheering**."
   "A **cheer** went up from the fans when our team won the game."

8. **score** (skôr)     *verb:* to make one or more points in a game
                              *noun:* A. the number of points each team has in a game
                                        B. the number of points a person receives on a test
   "Wayne is a terrific basketball player.  He **scored** 30 points last night."
   "Our baseball team is winning by a **score** of 5 to 1."

## Completing Sentences

**Complete the sentences with these words.** *Use each word twice. Where a word has different endings, both forms are given.*

crowd               score/scored               join/joined               cheers/cheered

1. The students _____ when the teacher said there would be no

   school tomorrow.

2. It was a rainy day, so the _____ at the parade was small.

3. Come in and _____ the party.

4. Our football team _____ 28 points; the other team had only 7.

5. The _____ were so loud we could hear them outside the gym.

6. The dancers _____ hands.

7. Kunio got a high _____ on his test.

8. The _____ is waiting for the theater to open.

## Creating Sentences

**Write an original sentence using these words.** *Work with a partner or on your own.*

5. (join) _____

6. (crowd) _____

7. (cheer) _____

8. (score) _____

# V.   STORY COMPLETION

**Discuss or think about these questions before completing the story that follows.**

1. Do you like football? Do you understand the game?
2. Did you ever go to a football game? Was it exciting?
3. Do you ever watch football on TV? How often?

Complete the story with these words.

| | | | |
|---|---|---|---|
| cheered | scored | fan | exciting |
| discovered | joined | crowd | amazed |

### A Football Star

My name is Doug Brown and I go to Hoboken High School. I'm a good student and a sports _____. I especially like football. Every Sunday afternoon and Monday night I watch professional football on TV. The New York Giants are my favorite team.

I like to play football, too, and I _____ our high school team in the beginning of September. The coach and the team soon _____ that I'm very fast, and now I play every game.

On Saturday we played an important game against Lincoln High School. They hadn't lost a game, and we had lost only one. There was a huge _____ at the game, and the fans _____ when we ran onto the field. Both teams thought that the game would be _____ and very close, but we _____ everyone by winning easily. I _____ 12 points and was the star of the game.

## VI.  SHARING INFORMATION

**Discuss these questions and topics in pairs or small groups.**

1. Are you a sports **fan**? If so, what sport or sports do you like?
2. When we travel, we're sometimes **amazed** by what we see. Name something that amazed you when you first saw it.
3. **Discover** often means *to find new information about a person or thing we already know*, for example, "Joe *discovered* that his friend was rich." Tell us what you discovered

    about a person or thing by completing this sentence: I discovered that _____

    _____.

4. Books, movies, and TV programs can be **exciting** or dull. Name a book, movie, or TV program that you found exciting and one that you found dull.

5. Did you ever **join** a team, club, or other group? If so, what team, club, or group did you join?

6. Many events and places attract **crowds,** for example, parades, important games, Niagara Falls. Name some other events or places that attract crowds.

7. In the United States, some sports have cheerleaders, young women or men who lead the **cheers** during a game. What sports usually have cheerleaders? What sports don't? Do other countries usually have cheerleaders?

8. In different sports, there are different names for the points a player **scores**; for example, players score *goals* in soccer. In what sport do they score *runs*? In what sport do they score *touchdowns*?

# VII. WORD FAMILIES

**Complete the sentences with these words.** *If necessary, add an ending to the word so it forms a correct sentence.* (adj. = adjective and adv. = adverb)

1. **amaze** (verb)   **amazing** (adj.)   **amazement** (noun)

   A. Computers work with _____ speed.

   B. You can imagine our _____ when Ralph hit his third home run

   in one game.

   C. New York City's skyscrapers (tall buildings) _____ visitors.

2. **discover** (verb)   **discovery** (noun)

   A. The _____ of oil helped the Mexican economy.

   B. I wasn't happy when I _____ that the dog ate my hamburger.

3. **exciting** (adj.)   **excite** (verb)
   **excited** (adj.)   **excitement** (noun)

   A. The children get _____ when they play.

   B. It's a quiet town with very little _____.

   C. The Olympic Games _____ most fans.

   D. I really enjoyed the play. It was _____.

159

4. **join** (verb)                    **joint** (adj.)

   A. My wife and I have a _____ checking account.

   B. Joan is going to _____ the band.  She likes music.

5. **crowd** (noun)                    **crowded** (adj.)

   A. The _____ was making so much noise that I couldn't hear what

      my friend was saying.

   B. The store is _____ because of the big sale.

6. **cheer** (verb or noun)            **cheerful** (adj.)
   **cheerfully** (adv.)              **cheerfulness** (noun)

   A. It's spring and the birds are singing _____.

   B. When the team heard the fans _____, they played harder.

   C. Ray is a _____ person.  He's always happy.

   D. The nurses' _____ helps the patients.

# VIII.  BUILDING WORDS WITH RE-

The prefix **re-** is placed before verbs to form a new verb.  For example, *re + write = rewrite; re + visit = revisit.*

The prefix **re-** means *again.  Rewrite* means *to write again; revisit* means *to visit again.*

| Verb | New Verb |
| --- | --- |
| build | rebuild |
| consider | reconsider |
| discover | rediscover |
| do | redo |
| enter | reenter |
| join | rejoin |
| marry | remarry |
| name | rename |

| | |
|---|---|
| open | reopen |
| play | replay |
| produce | reproduce |
| read | reread |
| visit | revisit |
| write | rewrite |

**Circle the letter next to the word that *best* completes the sentence.**

1. The store is closed, but it'll _____ in the morning.
   - a. reproduce
   - b. redo
   - c. revisit
   - d. reopen

2. Angela's husband died two years ago, but she's going to _____ soon.
   - a. remarry
   - b. reconsider
   - c. rebuild
   - d. rediscover

3. They decided to _____ the airport in honor of President Kennedy.
   - a. reenter
   - b. revisit
   - c. rename
   - d. reconsider

4. There are many mistakes in my letter. I'm going to _____ it.
   - a. replay
   - b. rewrite
   - c. rebuild
   - d. rediscover

5. We weren't able to spend much time at the museum. We're going to

   _____ it tomorrow.
   - a. revisit
   - b. reconsider
   - c. reproduce
   - d. rejoin

6. The fire completely destroyed the school, but the city is going to _____ it.
   - a. rejoin
   - b. reenter
   - c. rebuild
   - d. rediscover

7. Why don't you _____ the club? Everyone wants you to come back.
   - a. reproduce
   - b. rejoin
   - c. rename
   - d. redo

8. If you don't understand the story, you should _____ it.
   - a. rediscover
   - b. reopen
   - c. reenter
   - d. reread

161

# CHAPTER FOURTEEN
# *An Accident*

? ? ? ? ? ? ? ? ? ? ? ? ? ? ? ? ? ? ? ? ? ? ? ? ?

## PREVIEW QUESTIONS

**Discuss or think about these questions before reading the story.**

1. Were you ever in an auto accident?
2. How bad was it?
.3. What are some of the causes of auto accidents?

# An Accident

Connie is a **cautious** driver and never drives too fast. She loves to drive. However, she had an accident while she was driving back to her cousin's house after the soccer game. Mario, her cousins, and the children were talking about the game and how well Lou played. Everyone was having a good time when Connie stopped at a red light on Route 46.

**Suddenly** a big black Buick **crashed** into the back of their car. The driver had been drinking and was driving 70 miles an hour. He **attempted** to stop, but he reacted slowly and it was too late. After the crash the children began to cry and Connie felt weak. Fortunately, everyone in both cars was wearing seat belts, and no one was hurt.

Connie parked on the side of the highway, and everyone got out of the car. She asked the man for his license and registration and gave him hers. She could smell the liquor on his breath. While she was talking to him, one of her cousins hurried to a nearby diner and called the police.

They came in five minutes. They questioned Connie and the other driver and quickly discovered that he was drunk. He could hardly walk or talk. The accident was obviously his **fault**, so he couldn't **blame** Connie. The police wrote an accident report and called a taxi to take the other driver home. He was too drunk to drive.

The back of Connie and Mario's car was badly **damaged**. Of course, the other man's insurance company will have to pay for it. The **damage** to the Buick was **slight** because it was bigger and heavier. Connie was a little hesitant to drive, but she felt okay, so she got in the car and drove back to her cousin's.

They couldn't drive the car back to Chicago the way it was, so they brought it to a repair shop early the next day. The mechanic examined it and said it would cost $2,000 and take two days to repair. "But we want to start back to Chicago tonight," Connie reminded Mario. He said, "I know, but two more days in New Jersey won't kill us. Be grateful that no one was hurt, that it was a great wedding, and that we won the soccer game."

# I. COMPREHENSION QUESTIONS

## True or False

**If the sentence is true, write *T*.  If it's false, write *F* and change it to a true sentence.**

———— 1. Connie is a careless driver.

_____

———— 2. The passengers in her car were enjoying themselves.

_____

———— 3. The driver of the Buick tried to stop.

_____

———— 4. He was hurt.

_____

———— 5. Connie wouldn't give him her license and registration.

_____

———— 6. No one blamed Connie for the accident.

_____

———— 7. The Buick was badly damaged.

_____

———— 8. Connie wanted to leave for Chicago the day after the accident.

_____

## What Do You Think?

**Use your experience, judgment, and the story to answer these questions.** *The story alone won't answer them.*

1. Why do you think the driver of the Buick reacted slowly?
2. Why was it important to call the police?

3. Will Connie and Mario's insurance costs go up? Will the other driver's insurance costs go up? Explain your answers.

4. Why is it a good idea to drive again soon after an accident?

# II. WORD GUESSING

**Guess the meaning of the key words in these sentences.** *Use the context of the story and the sentences to guess. Circle your answers.*

1. Connie is a **cautious** driver and never drives too fast.

   a. very good
   b. very smart
   c. very careful
   d. very bad

2. The driver **attempted** to stop, but he reacted slowly and it was too late.

   a. wanted
   b. remembered
   c. had
   d. tried

3. The damage to the Buick was **slight** because it was bigger and heavier.

   a. small
   b. expensive
   c. interesting
   d. surprising

# III. MINI-DICTIONARY — PART ONE

## *Vocabulary Focus*

1. **cau·tious** (kô´shəs)    *adjective:* very careful
   "Alicia is **cautious**. She always thinks before she acts."

2. **sud·den·ly** (sud´ən-lē)    *adjective:* happening quickly
   "The truck in front of us stopped **suddenly**, and we almost hit it."

3. **crash** (krash)    *verb:* to hit with great force, especially in an accident
               *noun:* a violent accident in a car, plane, or train
   "The bus **crashed** into a telephone poll."
   "Three people were killed in the train **crash**."

4. **at·tempt** (ə-tempt´)    *verb:* to try; to make an effort
               *noun:* the act of trying
   "Sonia **attempted** to sell her car for $1,000."
   "I couldn't do my math homework, but at least I made an **attempt**."

## Completing Sentences

**Complete the sentences with these words.** *Use each word twice. Where a word has different endings, both forms are given.*

suddenly          attempt/attempting          cautious          crash/crashed

1. They're _____ to complete the highway by November 1, but I don't think they will.

2. Larry _____ felt sick and had to leave the room.

3. My friend was in a helicopter _____ , but he didn't get hurt.

4. Pablo is slow to change. He's _____ .

5. _____ it began to rain.

6. I thanked Emily for her _____ to get me a job.

7. My doctor is _____ . He wants me to rest a few days before I go back to work.

8. The baseball player _____ into the fence trying to catch the ball.

## Creating Sentences

**Write an original sentence using these words.** *Work with a partner or on your own.*

1. (cautious) _____

2. (suddenly) _____

3. (crash) _____

4. (attempt) _____

# IV.   MINI-DICTIONARY — PART TWO

## Vocabulary Focus

5. **fault** (fôlt)    *noun:*  A.  responsibility for something bad
                         B.  defect in a person or thing
       "It's my own **fault** that I did poorly on the exam.  I didn't study."

6. **blame** (blām)    *verb:* to hold someone responsible for something bad

                        *noun:* responsibility for something bad

    "The economy is doing poorly and many people **blame** the president."

    "Matthew is to **blame***  for the accident. He went through a red light."

    ***Blame** is frequently used in the expression *be to blame.*

7. **dam·age** (dam´ij)    *verb:* to make something less valuable; to harm

                        *noun:* loss of value; harm

    "Loud music can **damage** your hearing."

    "Hurricane Andrew did a lot of **damage** in Florida and Louisiana."

8. **slight** (slīt)    *adjective:* small; not serious

    "Kathleen has a **slight** cold. She'll be fine in a day or two."

## Completing Sentences

**Complete the sentences with these words.** *Use each word twice. Where a word has different endings, both forms are given.*

**slight**        **blame/blaming**        **damage/damaged**        **fault/faults**

1. The cold weather _____ the orange trees.

2. Jane is wonderful, but she has her _____ . She isn't perfect.

3. Masako speaks English well, but she has a _____ accent.

4. The food at the restaurant was terrible. I think the cook is to _____ .

5. We have to make some _____ changes in our plan.

6. How much _____ did the fire do to your house?

7. Ralph was late for work, but it wasn't his _____ . His car wouldn't start.

8. Why are they _____ me? I didn't do anything wrong.

## Creating Sentences

**Write an original sentence using these words.** *Work with a partner or on your own.*

5. (fault) _____

6. (blame) _____

7. (damage) _____

8. (slight) _____

# V.   STORY COMPLETION

**Discuss or think about these questions before completing the story that follows.**
1. Why should a person drive more slowly in the rain?
2. Why should a driver be careful when near trucks and buses?
3. Are you a cautious driver?

### Complete the story with these words.

| cautious | crashed | slight | damaged |
|---|---|---|---|
| attempted | blame | suddenly | fault |

### *Hitting a Bus in the Rain*

It was raining hard when the Greyhound bus left the station in San Francisco. The bus was going down a busy street when a car _____ to pass. That was a big mistake. The driver _____ lost control of his car and _____ into the side of the bus.

The accident wasn't the bus driver's _____. The driver of the car was to _____. He should have been more _____, but he was in a hurry and didn't want to stay behind the bus.

Fortunately, all the people on the bus were okay. So the driver got back in the bus and continued on her way to Los Angeles. However, the car was badly _____, and the driver had a _____ cut on his face. He had to call his wife to pick him up.

# VI.   SHARING INFORMATION

**Discuss these questions and topics in pairs or small groups.**
1. Which statement best describes you? A. I'm very **cautious**. B. I'm cautious. C. I'm a little cautious. D. I'm not at all cautious.
2. Tell us about something you did **suddenly**, or that suddenly happened to you.

3. When you get on a plane, how afraid are you of a **crash**?  A little?  A lot?  Not at all?  Which do you think is safer, flying or driving in a car?

4. Complete one of the following sentences:  I **attempted** to _____

   _____ , but couldn't.  I **attempted** to _____

   _____ and did.

5. No one is perfect.  We all have **faults**.  Think of a fault that you have or that a friend has, and tell us what it is.  For example, "My friend is lazy."

6. When a student does poorly in school, who is usually to **blame**?  The teacher(s)?  The student?  The parents?  No one?  Explain your answer.

7. Describe the **damage** caused by a fire, storm, or accident you were in or saw on television.

8. Some problems are big; some are **slight**:  Complete one of the following sentences:  I

   have a slight problem; _____ . My friend

   has a slight problem; _____ .

# VII.  WORD FAMILIES

**Complete the sentences with these words.**  *If necessary, add an ending to the word so it forms a correct sentence.*  (adj. = adjective and adv. = adverb)

1. **cautious** (adj.)          **caution** (noun)          **cautiously** (adv.)

   A. They removed the bomb from the building with great _____ .

   B. Dan spends his money _____ .

   C. It's not enough for firefighters to be brave.  They must also be _____ .

2. **suddenly** (adv.)          **sudden** (adj.)

   A. A _____ storm hit the coast of California.

   B. _____ the lights in our house went out.

3. **fault** (noun)          **faulty** (adj.)

   A. Kirk has his _____ , but he works hard.

   B. _____ wiring caused the fire.

169

4. **blame** (verb or noun)     **blameless** (adj.)

    A. The police made a mistake when they arrested Tony. He was

    _____ .

    B. Our team hasn't won a game, and I _____ the coach.

5. **slight** (adj.)     **slightly** (adv.)

    A. General Motors is offering its workers a _____ pay increase.

    B. It's _____ warmer today.

# VIII.  BUILDING ADJECTIVES WITH -OUS

The suffix **-ous** is added to nouns and verbs to form an adjective. For example, *fame + ous = famous*; *space + ous = spacious*; *religion + ous = religious*.

The suffix **-ous** usually means *having, having a lot of,* or *having to do with*. *Famous* means *having fame*; *spacious* means *having a lot of space*; *religious* means *having to do with religion*.

| Noun or Verb | Adjective |
|---|---|
| advantage | advantageous |
| caution | cautious |
| continue | continuous |
| fame | famous |
| joy | joyous |
| mountain | mountainous |
| mystery | mysterious |
| nerve | nervous |
| number | numerous |
| poison | poisonous |
| religion | religious |
| space | spacious |
| study | studious |

**Circle the letter next to the word that *best* completes the sentence.**

1. I love weddings. They're _____ occasions.
   - a. continuous
   - b. nervous
   - c. famous
   - d. joyous

2. I know Dallas well. I have made _____ trips there.
   - a. mysterious
   - b. numerous
   - c. advantageous
   - d. cautious

3. Jason is always in the library with his nose in a book. He's _____ .
   - a. studious
   - b. famous
   - c. religious
   - d. nervous

4. Much of Bolivia is _____ .
   - a. joyous
   - b. cautious
   - c. mountainous
   - d. continuous

5. That's _____ . My glasses were here a minute ago, and now I don't

   see them.
   - a. advantageous
   - b. continuous
   - c. mysterious
   - d. numerous

6. Almost everyone has heard of Babe Ruth. He was a _____ baseball

   player.
   - a. cautious
   - b. religious
   - c. nervous
   - d. famous

7. What a _____ room this is! You can put a lot in it.
   - a. spacious
   - b. mountainous
   - c. mysterious
   - d. continuous

8. Chris gets _____ when he has to go to a doctor.
   - a. joyous
   - b. nervous
   - c. religious
   - d. studious

# CHAPTER FIFTEEN

# A Pack a Day

## PREVIEW QUESTIONS

**Discuss or think about these questions before reading the story.**

1. Do you smoke?  A lot?
2. Why is it bad to smoke?
3. Why do people start smoking?

# A Pack a Day

Cigarette smoke contains carbon monoxide and other **dangerous** poisons. Smoking is the **main** cause of lung cancer. That's why there are **warnings** on the side of every pack of cigarettes and on all cigarette ads. One of them says, "Smoking causes lung cancer, heart disease, emphysema,* and may complicate pregnancy." Cigarette smoke is also dangerous for those who don't smoke, but who breathe air with cigarette smoke in it.

Although it's foolish to smoke, fifty million people in the United States still do. Most of them want to quit, but smoking is a habit that's not easy to break. Fortunately, thirty-five million Americans have stopped, so it can be done.

Mario **used to** smoke a pack of cigarettes a day. He started to smoke when he was 16. Many of his friends were doing it, and it made him feel like an adult. His parents told him he was making a mistake, but he didn't listen to them. When he joined the soccer team in the United States, he stopped smoking for two years, but then he started again.

A month ago, he had a **pain** in his chest and stomach. "The pain isn't too bad. I'm sure it'll go away and I'll be fine. I probably ate too much," he told Connie. But it didn't go away and they both began to **worry**. Mario called the doctor. He told him that Connie should drive him to the hospital **right away**. They checked his heart, took a chest x-ray, and kept him in the hospital overnight.

The next day his doctor read the x-ray report and the results of his other tests. He told Mario that he was okay, and that he could go back to work after a few days' rest. But he **warned** him to stop smoking. Mario and Connie were very happy. They were afraid that they were going to get bad news.

Mario stopped smoking immediately. He chews two packs of gum a day **instead** and feels much better. He doesn't cough in the morning the way he used to. His house and car don't smell of smoke, and his wife and children are breathing cleaner air.

---

*Emphysema** is a lung disease that makes it difficult to breathe.

# I. COMPREHENSION QUESTIONS

**Answer these questions about the story.** *Use your judgment to answer questions with an asterisk. Work in pairs or small groups. The numbers in parentheses show which paragraph in the story has the answer.*

1. What does cigarette smoke contain? (1)
2. Where will you find warnings about the dangers of smoking? (1)
3. Most smokers want to quit. Why don't they? (2)

4. Why did Mario start to smoke?  Give two reasons.  (3)

*5. Why does smoking make it difficult to play soccer?

6. Why did Mario and Connie begin to worry?  (4)

*7. Why did the doctor want Connie to drive and not Mario?

8. What did they do for Mario at the hospital?  (4)

9. What did the doctor tell him?  (5)

*10. What was the bad news they were afraid of?

11. What does Mario do instead of smoking?  (6)

12. Mario stopped smoking. Why was that good for the health of his wife and children?  (6)

## II.  WORD GUESSING

**Guess the meaning of the key words in these sentences.**  *Use the context of the story and the sentences to guess.  Circle your answers.*

1. Cigarette smoke contains carbon monoxide and other **dangerous** poisons.

    a. foolish          c. necessary

    b. dirty            d. unsafe

2. Smoking is *the* **main** cause of lung cancer.

    a. a common        c. the number one

    b. the only          d. a possible

3. Mario **used to** *smoke* a pack of cigarettes a day.

    a. is used to smoking      c. continues to smoke

    b. in the past smoked      d. enjoyed smoking

## III.  MINI-DICTIONARY — PART ONE

### Vocabulary Focus

1. **dan·ger·ous** (dān´jər-əs)  *adjective:* not safe; able or likely to do damage
   "The road is **dangerous**.  It's narrow and has many curves."

2. **main** (mān)  *adjective:* first in importance or size
   "In the United States, most people eat their **main** meal in the evening."

3. a. **warn** (wôrn)   *verb:* to say something is not safe or may cause a problem

"I **warned** the children not to play in the street."

   b. **warn·ing** (wôr´ning)   *noun:* a notice that something is not safe or may cause a problem

"The police officer gave me a **warning** not to drive so fast."

4. **used to** (yo͞os to͞o *or* yo͞os´tə)

*idiom:* done regularly in the past, but not now; true in the past, but not now

"Mi Sook **used to** live in Korea.  Now she lives in San Francisco."

## Completing Sentences

**Complete the sentences with these words.** *Use each word twice.  Where a word has different endings, both forms are given.*

| dangerous | main | warned/warning | used to |
| --- | --- | --- | --- |

1. Where is the _____ entrance to the school?

2. Texas _____ be part of Mexico.

3. Walking in the park late at night is _____.

4. The United States dropped the atomic bomb on Japan without _____.

5. The city has three libraries.  The _____ one is in the center of the city.

6. The teacher _____ us that the test would be hard.

7. Ellen is a firefighter.  Her job is _____.

8. I _____ play the piano.

## Creating Sentences

**Write an original sentence using these words.** *Work with a partner or on your own.*

1. (dangerous) _____

2. (main) _____

3. (warn) _____

4. (used to) _____

# IV. MINI-DICTIONARY — PART TWO

## Vocabulary Focus

5. **pain** (pān)    *noun:* very uncomfortable feeling;  suffering

    "The **pain** in my arm is bad.  I'm going to see a doctor."

6. **wor·ry** (wûr´ē)    *verb:* A. to think and feel something is dangerous or wrong
    B. to cause to think and feel this way

    *noun:* a feeling that something is dangerous or wrong; what causes this feeling

    "These big bills **worry** me."

    "When I play tennis, I forget my **worries**."

7. **right a·way** (rīt ə-wā´)    *adverb:* immediately; now

    "They sent an ambulance **right away**.  We didn't have to wait long."

8. **in·stead** (in-sted´)    *adverb:* in place of

    "We wanted to go swimming, but it was too cold.  So we went for a walk **instead**."

## Completing Sentences

**Complete the sentences with these words.** *Use each word twice.  Where a word has different endings, both forms are given.*

worry/worries            instead                pain                right away

1. Paula is very busy, but she answered my letter _____ .

2. Carl and Jean were going to play cards, but they watched TV _____ .

3. Hector plays football, and his mother _____ about his getting hurt.

4. Take some Tylenol, and the _____ will go away.

5. I don't like potatoes.  May I have some rice _____?

6. The show is going to start _____ .

7. Walter has a _____ in his back. He's going to stay home and rest.

8. I don't have a job and I can't find one. It's a big _____ .

## Creating Sentences

**Write an original sentence using these words.** *Work with a partner or on your own.*

5. (pain) _____

_____

6. (worry) _____

_____

7. (right away) _____

_____

8. (instead) _____

_____

# V. STORY COMPLETION

**Discuss or think about these questions before completing the story that follows.**

1. Do you like boxing? Do you ever watch it on TV?

2. Professional boxing is dangerous, for example, some boxers suffer brain damage. How can boxing be made safer?

3. Do you think the government should: A. stop all boxing? B. pass laws to make it safer? C. do nothing?

**Complete the story with these words.**

| main | instead | warned | pain |
|------|---------|--------|------|
| used to | worry | right away | dangerous |

### A Young Boxer

Tony Lanza ———————————— be a boxer, and he was one of the best young boxers in the state of Texas.  However, his parents didn't want him to box, and they ———————————— him to quit before he got hurt.  He knew that boxing was ———————————— , but he told his parents not to ————————————.  He was strong and healthy and loved to box.

One night, Tony was fighting a bigger and faster boxer.  It was an important fight for both boxers and the ———————————— fight of the evening.  Late in the fight, Tony got a bad cut over his left eye.  It was deep and the ———————————— was terrible.  He couldn't see out of his eye.  The referee stopped the fight ————————————.

Tony had planned to go to a victory party after he won the fight, but they had to take him to the hospital ————————————.  The doctors saved Tony's eye, but he's not going to box anymore.  His parents are very happy about that.

# V.  SHARING INFORMATION

**Discuss these questions and topics in pairs or small groups.**

1. Some sports are **dangerous**.  Others are safe.  Name three dangerous sports and three safe ones.
2. What is your **main** reason for studying English?  What are some other reasons?
3. Every pack of cigarettes and all cigarette ads **warn** people that smoking is dangerous.  Do these **warnings** help?  Do they keep some people from smoking?  Do they make others think about quitting?

4. Complete the following sentence:  I **used to** live in _____ ; now I live

in _____.

5. When we think of **pain**, we usually think of physical pain.  But pain can also be emotional or psychological.  Name some things that cause emotional or psychological pain, for example, losing a job.

6. Everyone **worries.**  Name three things people worry about.

7. When you wake up in the morning and it's time to get up, do you usually get up **right away**, or do you usually stay in bed a while?

8. Complete the following sentences: _____ is my favorite drink.  But if

I can't get it or want a change, I drink _____ **instead.**

# VII.  WORD FAMILIES

**Complete the sentences with these words.**  *If necessary, add an ending to the word so it forms a correct sentence.*  (adj. = adjective and adv. = adverb)

1. **dangerous** (adj.)        **danger** (noun)        **dangerously** (adv.)

   A.  If you put your money in the bank, there is very little _____

   of losing it.

   B.  That car came _____ close to us.

   C.  Arguing with the boss can be _____ .

2. **main** (adj.)                          **mainly** (adv.)

   A.  I like all kinds of music, but I'm _____ interested in rock.

   B.  Ms. Trawinsky is going to be the _____ speaker at the

   conference.

3. **pain** (noun)          **painful** (adj.)          **painless** (adj.)

   A.  I was lucky.  The tests I had in the hospital were _____ .

   B.  I have an earache, and the _____ is killing me.

   C.  Joy's sunburn is very _____ .

179

4. **instead** (adv.)                    **instead of** (preposition)

   A.  I was going to visit my cousin, but I phoned her _____ .

   B.  Lester is on a diet, so he ate an apple _____ a piece of cake.

# VIII.  BUILDING NOUNS WITH -ING

The suffix **-ing** is added to verbs to form a noun.  For example, *run + ing = running; read + ing = reading; paint + ing = painting.*

The suffix **-ing** means *the action of.*  For example, *running* means *the action of running; reading* means *the action of reading; painting* means *the action of painting.*

| Verb | Noun |
|------|------|
| begin | beginning |
| farm | farming |
| feel | feeling |
| hear | hearing |
| hunt | hunting |
| meet | meeting |
| paint | painting |
| read | reading |
| run | running |
| suffer | suffering |
| swim | swimming |
| understand | understanding |
| warn | warning |
| write | writing |

**Circle the letter next to the word that *best* completes the sentence.**

1. Pete is moving from the country to the city.  He doesn't like _____ .
        a.  swimming          c.  farming
        b.  running           d.  reading

2. You'll have to speak louder.  My _____ is poor.
        a.  beginning          c.  reading
        b.  hearing           d.  painting

3. Monica has a clear _____ of the problem and a plan to solve it.
        a.  understanding      c.  feeling
        b.  writing            d.  warning

4. The _____ of the play is very funny.
        a.  meeting          c.  painting
        b.  hunting           d.  beginning

5. I have a (an) _____ that it's going to snow.
        a.  hearing          c.  understanding
        b.  feeling           d.  reading

6. _____ is the most important skill children learn when they

start school.
        a.  reading          c.  farming
        b.  swimming        d.  painting

7. _____ is good exercise and fun.
        a.  meeting          c.  writing
        b.  understanding    d.  swimming

8. The teachers talked for three hours about ways to improve the school.  It was a long

_____ .
        a.  warning          c.  meeting
        b.  suffering        d.  beginning

# UNIT FIVE WORD REVIEW

## I.  SYNONYMS

Next to each sentence, write the word that has the same meaning or almost the same meaning as the part of the sentence in dark print.

| slight | cheered | attempting | main |
|--------|---------|------------|------|
| crowd  | suddenly | amazed     | cautious |

1. _____ When I drive in the snow, I'm **very careful**.

2. _____ The baby is **trying** to walk, but her legs aren't strong enough yet.

3. _____ A large **number of people** came to watch the parade.

4. _____ Danielle does a lot of things in the office, but her **most important** job is typing.

5. _____ Toyota announced a **small** increase in the price of their cars.

6. _____ We were **very surprised** that Brett spoke French, Italian, and Spanish.

7. _____ Everyone **shouted and clapped** when Michael Jackson began to sing.

8. _____ The door opened **quickly**.

## II.  SENTENCE COMPLETION

Complete the sentences with these words.

| fault | score | worry | damage |
|-------|-------|-------|--------|
| fans  | blame | exciting | warned |

1. My son is doing poorly in school, and I think his teacher is to _____ .

2. Shirley _____ me not to trust Jerry. I'm sorry I didn't listen to her.

3. We lost the game, but the _____ was close.

4. The children had a very _____ day at the zoo.

5. I have a headache, and it's my own _____ . I drank too much wine at the party.

6. Len enjoys life, and he doesn't _____ about anything.

7. Many _____ stayed home from the game because of the rain.

8. The students in our school don't pay for their books, but they have to return them at the end of the year and pay for any _____ .

# III.  STORY COMPLETION

**Complete the story with these words.**

| | | | |
|---|---|---|---|
| **dangerous** | **used to** | **crashed** | **pain** |
| **right away** | **discovered** | **instead** | **joining** |

### *Skiing*

Skiing is a _____ sport, and no one knows this better than Ivan.

He _____ ski a lot, but last winter he had a bad accident.

He was skiing down the side of a mountain, and he _____ into a tree. Ivan was in a lot of _____ , so they took him to a hospital _____ . They _____ that he had broken both of his legs.

This winter Ivan isn't going to do any skiing. He plans to swim _____ . He's _____ a local club where he can go swimming every day.

# UNIT SIX

# New Jobs for Women

# CHAPTER SIXTEEN
# *A Police Officer*

Illustration on chalkboard: A. FEDERAL LAW  B. STATE LAW  C. LOCAL LAW

? ? ? ? ? ? ? ? ? ? ? ? ? ? ? ? ? ? ? ? ? ? ? ? ?

## PREVIEW QUESTIONS

**Discuss or think about these questions before reading the story.**

1. Does the police department where you live have women police officers?  Many?
2. What do you think police officers have to learn before they start their job?
3. How do you think most parents feel about having a son or daughter join the police department?

# A Police Officer

When Nancy finished high school, she didn't want to go to college. Her parents said that was okay, but they didn't want her sitting around the house doing nothing. **Therefore**, she had to work or go to school. Since Nancy wanted to work and make some money, that was fine with her. She got a job at a bank and worked as a teller for four years. The job was interesting for a while because everything was new and she learned a lot.

Nancy, however, had always wanted to be a police officer. But she was only 17 when she graduated from high school, and that was too young. So she waited until she was 21. Then she made an **appointment** to talk to an officer at the police department.

Nancy was a little nervous when she talked to the officer, but he was kind and that helped her relax. He said the department didn't have any female police officers, but that she should **apply** and they would consider her. He warned her that the job was difficult and she would have to take both written and physical exams. She applied and did very well on the exams.

Six weeks later, she received an appointment to the police department. She was so excited she could hardly wait to tell her friends. Everyone at the bank wished her well and said they would miss her. Naturally, she was **eager** to begin, but first she had to go to the police academy for three months to learn about state and local laws, about the best way to handle people, and about how and when to use a gun. The academy was **rather** difficult, but Nancy completed her courses without much trouble.

Nancy's parents didn't like the idea of her becoming a police officer. They said that the job was too dangerous. They **suggested** that she become a computer programmer. She liked to work with computers and knew a lot about them. They would pay to send her to school to learn more, and then she could get a safe job.

Nancy **replied**, "I'm **aware** of the dangers, but I want to be a police officer, not a computer programmer. My job will be exciting and important. It'll give me a chance to help people and to make our streets a little safer. Besides, I'm 21 and it's my decision." But to her parents, she was still a little girl, and they were afraid.

# I. COMPREHENSION QUESTIONS

**Answer these questions about the story.** *Use your judgment to answer questions with an asterisk. Work in pairs or small groups. The numbers in parentheses show which paragraph in the story has the answer.*

1. What did Nancy's parents say about her not going to college? (1)
*2. Do you think they were unhappy about her not going to college? Explain your answer.
3. Why didn't Nancy become a police officer when she graduated from high school? (2)
4. Who did she make an appointment with? (2)
5. How did she feel when she talked to the officer? (3)
6. What warning did he give her? (3)
7. How did she feel when she learned about her appointment to the police department? (4)
8. Name three things they taught her in the police academy? (4)
9. What did Nancy's parents want her to become? (5)
*10. Do you think Nancy will have an opportunity to use her knowledge of computers in the police department? Explain your answer.
11. Why does she want to be a police officer? (6)
*12. Do you think she understands her parents' fears, or do you think she's angry at them? Explain your answer.

# II. WORD GUESSING

**Guess the meaning of the key words in these sentences.** *Use the context of the story and the sentences to guess. Circle your answers.*

1. Her parents didn't want her sitting around the house doing nothing. **Therefore**, she had to work or go to school.

   a. soon
   b. that's why
   c. but
   d. fortunately

2. Naturally, she *was* **eager** to begin, but first she had to go to the police academy.

   a. was foolish
   b. was slow
   c. was proud
   d. wanted very much

3. Nancy replied, "*I'm* **aware** *of* the dangers, but I want to be a police officer, not a computer programmer."

   a. I know about
   b. I'm unhappy about
   c. I'm afraid of
   d. I'm hesitant because of

# III. MINI-DICTIONARY — PART ONE

## Vocabulary Focus

1. **there·fore** (*thâr´fôr*)  *adverb:* for that reason; that is why; so
   "Tomorrow is a holiday. **Therefore**, I don't have to go to work."

2. **ap·point·ment** (ə-point´mənt)  *noun:*  A. an agreement to meet at a defi-
   nite time and place
   B. the placing of a person in a job
   "What time is your **appointment** with the doctor?"
   "Rita just received an **appointment** to teach history at Boston College."

3. **ap·ply** (ə-plī´)  *verb:* to ask for something formally, usually in writing
   "I'm **applying** for a Sears credit card."

4. **ea·ger** (to) (for) (ē´gər)  *adjective:* having a strong desire
   "Peggy is a good student. She's **eager** to learn."

## Completing Sentences

**Complete the sentences with these words.** *Use each word twice. Where a word has different endings, both forms are given.*

applying/applied              therefore              eager              appointment

1. Jeff has been in the hospital for ten days. He's _____ to go home.

2. Kim _____ for a visa to visit the United States, but she hasn't

   received it yet.

3. Mrs. Robinson is very busy. You have to have an _____ to see her.

4. Henry is rich. _____, he can buy almost anything he wants.

5. Carmen is calling the beauty salon for an _____.

6. The boss likes Stan because he's an _____ worker.

7. I'm on a diet. _____, I'm not having dessert.

8. Jackie wants to go to college, but her family doesn't have much money. She's

   _____ for financial aid.

189

## Creating Sentences

**Write an original sentence using these words.** *Work with a partner or on your own.*

1. (therefore) _____

   _____

2. (appointment) _____

   _____

3. (apply) _____

   _____

4. (eager) _____

   _____

# IV.  MINI-DICTIONARY — PART TWO

## Vocabulary Focus

5. **rath·er** (ra*th*´ər)   *adverb:* to some degree; quite
   "It's raining **rather** hard."

6. **sug·gest** (sə-jest´ *or* seg-jest´)   *verb:* to say that it is a good idea to do or consider something
   "Andy fell on the sidewalk and broke his leg.  I **suggested** that he see a lawyer."

7. **re·ply** (ri-plī´)   *verb:* to answer
   *noun:* an answer
   "I don't think the president will **reply** to that question."
   "We invited Amy and Dwight to our wedding, and we're waiting for a **reply**."

8. **a·ware** (of) (ə-wâr´)   *adjective:* having knowledge of
   "Are you **aware** that John and Cliff are good friends?"

## Completing Sentences

**Complete the sentences with these words.** *Use each word twice. Where a word has different endings, both forms are given.*

| aware | suggest/suggested | rather | reply/replied |
|---|---|---|---|

1. My doctor _____ that I lose 20 pounds and get more exercise.

2. I wasn't _____ that Mike liked to cook.

3. We asked the mayor to speak at our high school graduation, but he

   _____ that he was busy that night.

4. It's a big house, but the kitchen is _____ small.

5. Was Judy _____ that her son used drugs?

6. Can you _____ the name of a good restaurant near here?  We don't

   know where to eat.

7. This magazine is _____ interesting.  I like it.

8. I wrote to my sister two weeks ago, but I haven't received a _____ yet.

## Creating Sentences

**Write an original sentence using these words.** *Work with a partner or on your own.*

5. (rather) _____

   _____

6. (suggest) _____

   _____

7. (reply) _____

   _____

8. (aware) _____

   _____

# V.  STORY COMPLETION

**Discuss or think about these questions before completing the story that follows.**
  1. Do you like math?
  2. Do (did) you do well in math in school?
  3. Did a teacher ever call your parents?  If so, why?

### Complete the story with these words.

| | | | |
|---|---|---|---|
| applied | therefore | eager | rather |
| suggested | replies | appointment | aware |

### *Math and Marks*

Eric is in his last year in high school, and he hopes to graduate in June.  However, he did poorly on his first math test and worse on his second.  And both tests were _____ easy.  _____ , the math teacher phoned his parents and made a (an) _____ to see them.  Eric wasn't happy about the phone call or the meeting, but he knew it was his own fault that he was failing math.

Eric's parents and math teacher discussed the problem for an hour.  The teacher said that Eric wasn't paying attention in class and wasn't doing his homework.  She _____ that he spend an hour every night studying math.  When Eric's parents got home, they told him he had to pay attention in class and study more.  So he is spending a lot more time on his math, and his work is improving.

Eric is _____ to go to college, but his marks are below average.  He's _____ that it won't be easy to get into a good college.  He _____ to four colleges and hopes that one will take him.  He's waiting to receive their _____ .

192

# VI. SHARING INFORMATION

**Discuss these questions and topics in pairs or small groups.**

1. Complete this sentence: I want to learn more English; **therefore**, I _____

   _____ .

2. How do you make an **appointment** to see a doctor or dentist? How long do you usually have to wait to get an appointment? If you don't have a doctor or dentist, how would you choose one?

3. When you **apply** for a job, you have to fill out an application. Job applications always ask for your name, address, and phone number. What other questions do they usually ask?

4. Complete this sentence: I'm **eager** to _____

   _____ .

5. **Rather** means *to some degree*; **very** means *to a high degree*. Complete these sentences with *rather* or *very:*

   1. It's _____ cold in Alaska in the winter.

   2. Bert is six feet tall. He's _____ tall.

   3. This dress costs $300. It's _____ expensive.

   4. I have to walk a mile to school. That's _____ far.

6. Anne has to buy a car and has $5,000 in the bank. She can buy a used car for $5,000, or get a loan and buy a new one costing much more. Which would you **suggest**? Explain your answer.

7. When you get an invitation, letter, or other mail that requires a **reply**, do you usually reply quickly, or do you wait until you have to reply?

8. Complete this statement: Most people aren't **aware** that I _____

   _____ . Or complete this question:

   Are you **aware** that I _____

   _____ ?

# VII. WORD FAMILIES

**Complete the sentences with these words.** *If necessary, add an ending to the word so it forms a correct sentence.* (adj. = adjective and adv. = adverb)

1. **appointment** (noun)            **appoint** (verb)

   A. The company is going to _____ a new president soon.

   B. Otto and his wife have an _____ to see a marriage counselor.

2. **apply** (verb)            **application** (noun)            **applicant** (noun)

   A. I filled out a job _____ and gave it to the secretary.

   B. The college has so many _____ that it can accept only

   30 percent of them.

   C. Ron is _____ to become a member of our club.

3. **eager** (adj.)            **eagerly** (adv.)            **eagerness** (noun)

   A. It has been a long winter, and we're _____ waiting for

   spring.

   B. I was in the hospital for a month, and the skill of the nurses and their

   _____ to help were great.

   C. Sheila and Elliot are _____ to move into their new house.

4. **suggest** (verb)            **suggestion** (noun)

   A. I was talking to the music teacher after class, and she _____

   that I take piano lessons.

   B. We don't know where to go on our vacation. Do you have any

   _____ ?

5. **aware** (adj.)                                **awareness** (noun)

    A. The discussion increased the students' _____ of the advantages of a college education.

    B. I hope you're _____ of the dangers of drinking and driving.

# VIII.   BUILDING WORDS WITH IN-

The prefix **in-** is placed before adjectives and nouns to form a new word. For example, *in + correct = incorrect; in + dependent = independent.*

The prefix **in-** means *not*. *Incorrect* means *not correct*; *independent* means *not dependent*.

| Adjective or Noun | New Word |
|---|---|
| active | inactive |
| complete | incomplete |
| correct | incorrect |
| definite | indefinite |
| dependent | independent |
| direct | indirect |
| expensive | inexpensive |
| experience | inexperience |
| formal | informal |
| frequent | infrequent |
| human | inhuman |
| secure | insecure |
| sufficient | insufficient |
| visible | invisible |

**Circle the letter next to the word that *best* completes the sentence.**

1. Mary Lou does whatever she wants. She's an _____ person.
   - a. inactive
   - b. independent
   - c. insecure
   - d. invisible

2. Arnold didn't finish his report. It's _____ .
   - a. incorrect
   - b. informal
   - c. indefinite
   - d. incomplete

3. The governor doesn't believe in the death penalty. He thinks it's

   _____ .
   - a. inhuman
   - b. insufficient
   - c. infrequent
   - d. inactive

4. I don't have a lot of money, so I'm going to buy an _____ watch.
   - a. incorrect
   - b. indirect
   - c. inexpensive
   - d. invisible

5. It's an _____ restaurant. You don't need a tie or jacket.
   - a. informal
   - b. incomplete
   - c. independent
   - d. indefinite

6. The little girl cries when her mother leaves her. She's _____ .
   - a. incorrect
   - b. inactive
   - c. indirect
   - d. insecure

7. We need more food for the picnic. What we have is _____.

      a. inhuman               c. insufficient

      b. incorrect            d. infrequent

8. The teacher said my answer was _____, but I still think it's right.

      a. indirect              c. indefinite

      b. incorrect            d. inactive

# CHAPTER SEVENTEEN

# Help! Help!

## PREVIEW QUESTIONS

**Discuss or think about these questions before reading the story.**
1. Do you like to walk in the park?
2. Is it safe to walk in most parks during the day? At night?
3. Do you trust most people? Or only a few?

# *Help! Help!*

Paula Romano teaches the third grade at number six school. She left school at 3:30 and decided to go for a short walk in the park before going home. It was a warm spring day and Paula was tired. She sat on a park bench to relax. She was enjoying the **mild** weather and watching the children play baseball. There wasn't a cloud in the sky.

A tall, thin man **approached** Paula. She's very friendly and trusts everyone. She looked up and smiled; she wasn't afraid. The man didn't smile, but asked her what time it was. When she looked at her watch, he took her handbag. He was a **thief.**

He had a gun and **threatened** to shoot Paula if she called for help. She was smart enough to keep quiet while he was near. She had only $20 dollars in her handbag, but she had a lot of credit cards, all of her keys, and some important papers in it. And she was angry.

She waited about ten seconds as the thief ran away. Then she shouted, "Help! help! That man is **stealing** my handbag!" A man who was jogging heard her and **chased** the thief, but it was too late. The thief was fast. There was a phone not far from the bench where Paula had been sitting. The jogger gave her 20¢, and she called the police.

Nancy, the new police officer, received the call for help, but by the time she **reached** the park, the thief was gone. Nancy **recognized** Paula immediately. Paula was Nancy's third grade teacher. Nancy gave Paula a big hug and asked her to describe the thief. "He was wearing a blue jacket and gray pants. He's quite tall and has long brown hair. I can still see his face. I will recognize him if I see him again," Paula said. "Don't worry, Mrs. Romano," Nancy replied. "We'll get him and we'll get your handbag back."

Nancy and Paula rode around the neighborhood looking for the thief. After about an hour, Paula suddenly saw a man in a blue jacket coming out of a bar. It was the thief. Nancy found the handbag in the man's car, so she arrested him and took him to the police station. He's in jail now and Paula is happy to have her keys and papers back. And, of course, she's proud of her third grade student.

# I. COMPREHENSION QUESTIONS

## True or False

**If the sentence is true, write *T*. If it's false, write *F* and change it to a true statement.**

_____ 1. After school, Paula went for a walk in the park.

_____

_____ 2. She didn't trust the tall, thin man who asked for the time.

_____

_____ 3. The thief said he would shoot Paula if she called for help.

_____

_____ 4. She had a lot of money in her handbag.

_____

_____ 5. A police officer heard her shout for help and chased the thief.

_____

_____ 6. Nancy had a special reason for hugging Paula.

_____

_____ 7. Nancy said she would catch the thief and return Paula's handbag.

_____

_____ 8. The thief threw away her handbag.

_____

## What Do You Think?

**Use your experience, judgment, and the story to answer these questions.** *The story alone won't answer them.*

1. Do you think Paula will trust others less in the future? Explain your answer.
2. Why was it especially important for Paula to get her keys back?
3. What should a person do if he or she loses a credit card(s)?
4. Do you think it was foolish for the jogger to chase the thief? Explain your answer.

# II.  WORD GUESSING

**Guess the meaning of the key words in these sentences.** *Use the context of the story and the sentences to guess.  Circle your answers.*

1. A tall, thin man **approached** Paula.
   - a. looked at
   - b. offered to help
   - c. came up to
   - d. talked to

2. Then she shouted, "Help! help!  That man is **stealing** my handbag!"
   - a. opening
   - b. damaging
   - c. searching
   - d. taking

3. A man who was jogging heard her and **chased** the thief, but it was too late.
   - a. stopped
   - b. ran after
   - c. caught
   - d. fought with

# III.  MINI-DICTIONARY — PART ONE

## Vocabulary Focus

1. **mild** (mīld)　*adjective:* gentle;  not strong or bitter;  not serious
   "Florida has hot summers and **mild** winters."

2. **ap·proach** (ə-prōch´)　*verb:* to come near
   　　　　　　　*noun:* A.  the act of coming near
   　　　　　　　　　　　B.  the way leading to a city, bridge, etc.
   　　　　　　　　　　　C.  a way of doing things
   "The plane is **approaching** the airport."
   "I can't wait for the end of winter and the **approach** of spring."

3. **thief** (thēf)　*noun:* a person who takes things that belong to another
   "The **thief** entered the house through a window.  The doors were locked."

4. **threat·en** (thret´ən)　*verb:* to say or show you will punish or hurt in
   　　　　　　　　　　　　　some way
   "I may lose my job.  The manager **threatened** to fire me."

201

## Completing Sentences

**Complete the sentences with these words.** *Use each word twice. Where a word has different endings, both forms are given.*

approach/approaches        mild        threatens/threatened        thief

1. Dorothy has a _____ case of the flu. It's nothing to worry about.

2. I want a pay increase, but I'm afraid to _____ the boss.

3. A _____ broke into my apartment and took my stereo and TV.

4. Sometimes Robin's teacher _____ to send her to the principal. She

   talks too much and doesn't do any work.

5. I like this cheese. It's _____ .

6. Was your son serious when he _____ to leave home?

7. I didn't take your money. I'm not a _____ .

8. The soldiers are guarding the _____ to the city.

## Creating Sentences

**Write an original sentence using these words.** *Work with a partner or on your own.*

1. (mild) _____

2. (approach) _____

3. (thief) _____

4. (threaten) _____

# IV.  MINI-DICTIONARY — PART TWO

## Vocabulary Focus

    5. **steal** (stēl)    *verb:* to take what belongs to another
       "Never leave money in your desk. Someone may **steal** it."
       The past of **steal** is **stole.**

6. **chase** (chās)    *verb:* to run after to catch

          *noun:* the act of chasing

"The cat is **chasing** a mouse."

"The police caught the man after a long **chase**."

7. **reach** (rēch)    *verb:* A. to arrive at; to come to

               B. to extend one's arm and hand to touch or get something

          *noun:* the distance a person can reach

"It took us four hours to **reach** the top of the mountain."

"Don't put the medicine within **reach** of the children."

8. **rec·og·nize** (rek´əg-nīz)    *verb:* to know a person or thing because of previous knowledge of him, her, or it

"Ken had not seen Virginia for 20 years, but he **recognized** her immediately."

## Completing Sentences

**Complete the sentences with these words.** *Use each word twice. Where a word has different endings, both forms are given.*

**reach/reached**        **steals/stole**        **chase/chased**        **recognize/recognized**

1. Brian _____ the baseball after it went over his head.

2. It was very dark, but I _____ my friend's voice.

3. They broke into the office last night and _____ two typewriters and our computer.

4. Can you get the flour for me? I can't _____ that high.

5. My dog likes to _____ rabbits and squirrels.

6. I left my bicycle in the yard. I hope no one _____ it.

7. We left New York City at 10:00 in the morning and _____ Washington at 2:00 in the afternoon.

8. We have made so many changes in our apartment. You won't _____ it.

## Creating Sentences

**Write an original sentence using these words.** *Work with a partner or on your own.*

5. (steal) _____

6. (chase) _____

7. (reach) _____

8. (recognize) _____

# V.   STORY COMPLETION

**Discuss or think about these questions before completing the story.**
1. Did anyone ever steal anything from you?
2. What did the person steal and from where?
3. Did you get back what was stolen?

### Complete the story with these words.

| recognize | chases | mild | approaching |
|-----------|--------|------|-------------|
| threaten | thieves | reach | steal |

### Robbing a Bank

Alex and Sam are professional _____. They'll

_____ anything, but they prefer money and expensive

cars.  They haven't stolen anything for a while, however.  Alex had a

_____ heart attack about six weeks ago, and the doctor told him to

get more rest.  He's going back to work today.

Alex and Sam are _____ the entrance to the First

National Bank and are putting on their ski masks.   They don't want anyone to

_____ them.

They walk up to two bank tellers, _____ into their pockets, and pull out their guns.  They make the tellers fill two bags with cash and

_____ to shoot anyone who calls for help.  They take the money

and run out of the bank.  A bank guard _____ them, but they jump

into their car and drive away before he can stop them.

# VI.   SHARING INFORMATION

**Discuss these questions and topics in pairs or small groups.**

1. Onions, pepper, and garlic make food hot and spicy.  Do you like spicy food, or do you like food that's **mild**?

2. Some people are easy to **approach**; others are difficult to approach.  What makes a person easy to approach?  What makes a person difficult to approach?

3. What do banks do to protect themselves and their tellers from **thieves** like Alex and Sam?

4. Parents frequently **threaten** their children.  For example, they say, "If you don't clean your room, you can't watch TV tonight."  Give another example of a threat parents make.  What happens if parents threaten a lot and then do nothing when their children don't listen?

5. To **steal** usually means to take a thing that belongs to another, but people also steal ideas.  Give an example of stealing ideas.

6. Movies and TV shows often have **chases**, especially car chases.  These chases are exciting and many end in crashes.  Describe a typical chase that you see in the movies or on TV.

7. What are some things that parents should lock up, or put in a place where small children can't **reach** them?

8. If you met someone who hadn't seen you for many years, for example, your first grade teacher or an old friend, do you think that person would **recognize** you?  Or have you changed too much for that?

# VII.   WORD FAMILIES

**Complete the sentences with these words.**  *If necessary, add an ending to the word so it forms a correct sentence.*  (adj. = adjective and adv. = adverb)

1. **mild** (adj.)                              **mildly** (adv.)

   A.  Roy had a _____ headache.

   B.  I was only _____ interested in Sue's story.

2. **approach** (verb and noun)        **approachable** (adj.)

   A. We like our supervisor. She's very _____.

   B. Our math teacher is trying a new _____ this year.

3. **threaten** (verb)                **threat** (noun)

   A. Mrs. Morales _____ to keep her class after school.

   B. Everyone had to leave the building because of a bomb _____.

4. **recognize** (verb)               **recognition** (noun)

   A. Doris works very hard for the company. She should get more _____

   and a pay increase.

   B. When I saw Dick's picture in the paper, I _____ him immediately.

# VIII.   BUILDING VERBS WITH -EN

The suffix **-en** is added to adjectives and nouns to form a verb. For example, *fright + en = frighten; sweet + en = sweeten; threat + en = threaten.*

The suffix **-en** means *to cause, to cause to be,* or *to make. Frighten* means *to cause fright; sweeten* means *to cause to be sweet; threaten* means *to make a threat.*

| Adjective or Noun | Verb |
| --- | --- |
| dark | darken |
| deep | deepen |
| fright | frighten |
| hard | harden |
| length | lengthen |
| less | lessen |
| sad | sadden |
| short | shorten |
| sick | sicken |
| soft | soften |
| sweet | sweeten |
| threat | threaten |
| weak | weaken |

**Circle the letter next to the word that _best_ completes the sentence.**

1. Exercise will _____ your body.
   - a. deepen
   - b. strengthen
   - c. sweeten
   - d. shorten

2. The road is narrow, but there are plans to _____ it.
   - a. widen
   - b. harden
   - c. darken
   - d. lengthen

3. The death of our friend _____ us.
   - a. softened
   - b. shortened
   - c. deepened
   - d. saddened

4. The field is dry and hard; we need some rain to _____ it.
   - a. lengthen
   - b. weaken
   - c. soften
   - d. deepen

5. What do they put in diet soda to _____ it?
   - a. sweeten
   - b. darken
   - c. harden
   - d. lessen

6. The loud noise _____ the dog and she ran away.
   - a. weakened
   - b. sickened
   - c. saddened
   - d. frightened

7. If you put the ice cream in the freezer, it'll _____ quickly.
   - a. lengthen
   - b. darken
   - c. harden
   - d. deepen

8. The play is too long.  The director should _____ it.
   - a. soften
   - b. shorten
   - c. weaken
   - d. widen

# CHAPTER EIGHTEEN
# *A Lot of Courage*

???????????????????????

## PREVIEW QUESTIONS

**Discuss or think about these questions before reading the story.**

1. Tell what you expect of a good police officer by completing this sentence: A good

   police officer should _____.

2. Some policemen have difficulty accepting women police officers. Why do you think this is so?

3. What are the advantages of having women police officers? Do you think there are any disadvantages?

# A Lot of Courage

Nancy was the first female police officer in Gary, Indiana. Many in town **wondered** if she would be a good police officer. They asked themselves a lot of questions. Was she strong enough? Was she old enough? And then there was the biggest question of all. Would the other police officers accept her? Before they hired Nancy, jobs in the police department were for men only.

One policeman said, "I like to watch policewomen on TV shows, but I don't think they're **tough** enough to do the job in the real world." Nancy was aware of what people were saying and thinking, but it didn't **bother** her. She knew she could do the job.

**At first**, Nancy's **partner** Dave didn't like the idea of working with a woman, but he doesn't feel that way now. One night Dave and Nancy were working in a dangerous part of town, and he attempted to arrest a man selling drugs. The drug dealer took Dave's gun and was going to shoot him. Nancy was 30 feet away and didn't hesitate. She shot the dealer and saved Dave's life.

When Dave returned to the police station, he said to the captain, "Nancy is one of our best police officers. She has a lot of **courage** and isn't afraid of danger. She's willing to take **risks**, but doesn't take foolish ones. She saved my life."

Nancy also works well with the other police officers. She smiles and laughs easily and is always pleasant. That makes it easy for them to accept her. However, she knows how to be tough, and sometimes her job requires it. She's a **successful** police officer because she knows when to be kind and when to be tough. She knows when to stop a car and give the driver a ticket, and when to give a warning instead. She knows when to use her gun and when not to. She does not like to use force, but uses it when necessary.

Nancy loves her job and never misses work, but her mom and dad still worry about her. They don't relax until she gets home, and they know she's safe. But they also see how happy she is and that she's a good police officer. People don't ask questions and don't wonder about her anymore, and, of course, her parents are proud of her **success**.

# I. COMPREHENSION QUESTIONS

**Answer these questions about the story.** *Use your judgment to answer questions with an asterisk. Work in pairs or small groups. The numbers in parentheses show which paragraph in the story has the answer.*

1. What did many people in town wonder? (1)
2. What three questions did they ask themselves? (1)
3. Why didn't the policeman think that women would make good police officers? (2)
*4. Who do you think told Nancy what people were saying and thinking?

*5. Why do you think Dave didn't want to work with Nancy?

6. What happened when he attempted to arrest a drug dealer? (3)

7. Why does he say that Nancy is one of their best police officers? (4)

*8. How much do you think police officers worry about the risks they must take? A lot? A little? Not at all?

9. What makes it easy for the other police officers to accept Nancy? (5)

10. Why is she a successful police officer? (5)

11. How does she feel about her job? (6)

12. When do her parents relax? (6)


# II.  WORD GUESSING

**Guess the meaning of the key words in these sentences.** *Use the context of the story and the sentences to guess. Circle your answers.*

1. One policeman said, "I like to watch policewomen on TV shows, but I don't think they're **tough** enough to do the job in the real world."

|   |   |   |   |
|---|---|---|---|
| a. smart | | c. big | |
| b. fast | | d. strong and hard | |

2. Nancy was aware of what people were saying and thinking, but it didn't **bother** *her.*

|   |   |   |   |
|---|---|---|---|
| a. disturb her | | c. make her quit | |
| b. interest her | | d. make her happy | |

3. Nancy *has a lot of* **courage** and isn't afraid of danger.

|   |   |   |   |
|---|---|---|---|
| a. is very polite | | c. can do what's very difficult | |
| b. is very careful | | d. is very friendly | |


# III.  MINI-DICTIONARY — PART ONE

## *Vocabulary Focus*

1. **won·der** (wun´dər)    *verb:* to be uncertain and want to know; to ask oneself

   *noun:* A. a person or thing that is extraordinary

   B. the feeling of surprise and respect that comes from seeing the extraordinary

   "I **wonder** what happened to my old friend George."

   "Niagara Falls is one of the **wonders** of the world."

2. **tough** (tuf)    *adjective:*  A.  strong and able to do what is difficult

    B.  difficult to do

"Boxers and football players have to be **tough.**"

3. **both·er** (both´ər)    *verb:*  A.  to disturb; to take away one's peace

    B.  to concern oneself about; to make an effort to

    *noun:* a person or thing that disturbs one

"It really **bothers** me when the children don't listen."

"I'll watch your daughter while you go to the store.  She's no **bother.**"

4. **at first** (at fûrst)    *idiom:*  in the beginning

"Our math course was easy **at first**, but now it's difficult."

## Completing Sentences

**Complete the sentences with these words.**  *Use each word twice.  Where a word has differ-ent endings, both forms are given.*

| at first | wonder/wondered | bother/bothers | tough |
| --- | --- | --- | --- |

1. I _____ what time it is.

2. Our boss is kind, but she can also be _____ .

3. Don't _____ to cook dinner.  We'll eat out tonight.

4. The play was dull _____ , but it became interesting.

5. That was a _____ test.  I'm glad that I studied for it.

6. Craig _____ how much the bicycle cost.

7. The water felt cold _____ , but it feels fine now.

8. My little sister _____ me a lot, but I try to be nice to her.

## Creating Sentences

**Write an original sentence using these words.** *Work with a partner or on your own.*

1. (wonder) _____

2. (tough) _____

3. (bother) _____

4. (at first) _____


# IV.  MINI-DICTIONARY — PART TWO

## Vocabulary Focus

5. **part·ner** (pärt´nər)  *noun:* a person who works, lives, or shares an activity with another

   "The dance is going to begin.  Does everyone have a **partner?**"

6. **cour·age** (kûr´ij)  *noun:* ability to do what is dangerous or painful

   "You need **courage** to be a good soldier."

7. **risk** (risk)  *noun:* danger;  possibility of loss

   *verb:* to place in danger

   "There's very little **risk** when you put your money in the bank."

   "Firefighters **risk** their lives to save people."

8. a. **suc·cess** (sək-ses´)  *noun:* the accomplishing of one's aim;  anything that goes well

   "The party was a big **success**.  Everyone had a good time."

   b. **suc·cess·ful** (sək-ses´fəl)  *adjective:* having accomplished one's aim;  having gone well

   "Ernie works hard.  That's why he's a **successful** businessman."

## Completing Sentences

**Complete the sentences with these words.** *Use each word twice.  Where a word has different endings, both forms are given.*

| courage | success/successful | partner/partners | risk/risks |
|---------|--------------------|-----------------|------------|

1. My friend had a serious operation. Fortunately, it was a _____.

2. Amanda is a good driver. She doesn't take unnecessary _____.

3. It takes _____ to quit smoking.

4. Fred and Al own and run a restaurant. They're _____.

5. Too much weight and too little exercise increase the _____ of a

   heart attack.

6. Tracy is a _____ writer. Her books are very popular.

7. One of the most important things in life is the choice of a marriage

   _____.

8. It takes a lot of skill and _____ to be an astronaut.

## Creating Sentences

**Write an original sentence using these words.** *Work with a partner or on your own.*

5. (partner) _____

6. (courage) _____

7. (risk) _____

8. (success) _____

9. (successful) _____

# V.   STORY COMPLETION

**Discuss or think about these questions before completing the story.**

1. What are some of the advantages of owning your own business?
2. What are some of the disadvantages?
3. What would a person have to do to open a store?

Complete the story with these words.

courage          success          bothered          tough

risk             partners         at first          wondered

## Their Own Business

Brenda and her friend Lucy used to work at a stationery store. They liked their work and they liked Henry, the owner of the store. He was pleasant and easy to work for, but he didn't pay them much. They weren't happy about their pay, and they _____ if they should open their own store. They realized they might make a lot of money, or lose a lot. It would be a big _____.

Brenda was eager to open a new store. _____ Lucy didn't like the idea, but she changed her mind. They told Henry they were going to quit and open their own store. This took _____. Henry listened carefully and wished them well. He wasn't happy, but he tried not to show how much their decision _____ him.

Brenda and Lucy became business _____, and they soon discovered how _____ it is to start your own business. They had to borrow money, fix the store, buy supplies, advertise, keep records, and work long hours. They're going to open their store next week. Brenda, Lucy, and their friends hope their store will be a _____, but they can't be sure.

# VI.  SHARING INFORMATION

**Discuss these questions and topics in pairs or small groups.**

1.  Complete two of the following sentences:  I **wonder** where _____ .

    I **wonder** if _____ .  I **wonder** how much _____ .

2.  Name something you did or something you're doing that's **tough** to do.

3.  Name some ways in which students **bother** teachers.

4.  Complete the following sentences:  I started to learn English _____

    ago.  **At first** _____ .

5.  Married couples are **partners**, and love is the most important thing in this partnership.
    But it's not the only important thing.  How important is it for marriage partners to share
    common interests, to like to do and talk about the same things?  Explain your answer.

6.  Some say **courage** is to act without fear in a dangerous situation.  Others say that
    courage is to do what is dangerous although we're afraid.  What do you think?

7.  We cannot live without taking **risks**.  Name some ordinary risks we take with little or
    no worry.

8.  Everyone wants to be a **success**.  What do you think *you* have to do to be a success in life?

# VII.  WORD FAMILIES

**Complete the sentences with these words.**  *If necessary, add an ending to the word so it
forms a correct sentence.*  (adj. = adjective and adv. = adverb)

1.  **wonder** (verb or noun)         **wonderful** (adj.)

    A.  That was a great dinner.  You're a _____ cook!

    B.  I _____ where I left my wallet.

2.  **partner** (noun)         **partnership** (noun)

    A.  Ralph and I often study together.  We're study _____ .

    B.  Linda and Cathy are forming a _____ .  They're lawyers.

3. **courage** (noun)  **courageous** (adj.)  **encourage** (verb)
   **encouragement** (noun)  **discourage** (verb)  **discouragement** (noun)

   A. Banks _____ everyone to save money.

   B. Gandhi was a _____ leader who helped India win independence.

   C. High prices _____ people from buying homes.

   D. Jennifer has been sick for two weeks and isn't improving. Her _____

   is understandable.

   E. It took _____ to tell the president that he was wrong.

   F. Our team is losing badly. The players need some _____ from

   their fans.

4. **risk** (noun or verb)  **risky** (adj.)

   A. Every time you get in a car, there's a slight _____ .

   B. The roads are covered with ice. It's too _____ to drive.

5. **success** (noun)  **succeed** (verb)  **unsuccessful** (adj.)

   A. If at first you don't _____ , try again.

   B. I was _____ in my attempt to run a mile in five minutes.

   C. The concert was a _____ . It made money and everyone

   enjoyed the music.

# VIII.  BUILDING ADJECTIVES WITH -ING

The suffix **-ing** is added to verbs to form an adjective.  For example, *excite + ing = exciting;*
*understand + ing = understanding.*

The suffix **-ing** adds no special meaning to the verb.

| Verb | Adjective |
|------|-----------|
| amaze | amazing |
| come | coming |
| die | dying |
| encourage | encouraging |
| excite | exciting |
| follow | following |
| interest | interesting |
| last | lasting |
| love | loving |
| miss | missing |
| open | opening |
| will | willing |
| win | winning |
| understand | understanding |

**Circle the letter next to the word that *best* completes the sentence.**

1. The election was close and very _____ .
   - a. understanding
   - b. exciting
   - c. loving
   - d. lasting

2. They've looked everywhere for the _____ child, but they can't find her.
   - a. willing
   - b. amazing
   - c. interesting
   - d. missing

3. I got some _____ news from my doctor.  I'm well enough to leave
   the hospital.
   - a. loving
   - b. lasting
   - c. encouraging
   - d. winning

4. You have an hour to answer the _____ questions.

    a. following             c. coming

    b. amazing            d. willing

5. The _____ chapter of the book is the best.

    a. understanding     c. loving

    b. winning            d. opening

6. They're going to cut down the _____ trees and plant new ones.

    a. willing             c. lasting

    b. dying              d. exciting

7. If you have the _____ numbers in this week's lottery, you'll be rich.

    a. winning           c. missing

    b. amazing          d. interesting

8. Hiroshi always has time to listen to his children. He's a (an) _____ father.

    a. missing           c. understanding

    b. lasting            d. exciting

## I. SYNONYMS

Next to each sentence, write the word that has the same meaning or almost the same meaning as the part of the sentence in dark print.

| tough | reply | rather | approaching |
|-------|-------|--------|-------------|
| stole | risk  | chase  | bothers     |

1. _____ I don't let my son swim alone. There's too much **danger**.

2. _____ We're **getting close to** the bridge.

3. _____ Mrs. Lopez works full time and has three young children. That's **difficult**.

4. _____ Throw the stick. The dog will **run to get** it and bring it back.

5. _____ Someone **took** Eva's coat.

6. _____ May I have a glass of water, please? I'm **quite** thirsty.

7. _____ Our math teacher won't let us talk in class. It **disturbs** her.

8. _____ Ryan wrote to his parents to ask for money. He hopes they'll **answer** soon.

## II.  SENTENCE COMPLETION

### Complete the sentences with these words.

| applied | thieves | recognize | partner |
|---------|---------|-----------|---------|
| threatened | appointment | mild | suggested |

1. Mr. Martini is a good lawyer, but you have to wait three weeks for an _____

   to see him.

2. Pam _____ that we go to the beach tomorrow.  What do you think?

3. The police officer _____ to give me a ticket for driving too fast.

4. Lisa and her _____ run the gift shop on the corner.

5. Car _____ know how to get into locked cars.

6. This drink tastes good, and it's _____ .

7. Do you _____ the woman in the red dress?

8. I _____ for a loan yesterday.  I hope I get it.

## III.  STORY COMPLETION

### Complete the story with these words.

| aware | therefore | reach | wondered |
|-------|-----------|-------|----------|
| success | at first | courage | eager |

### *Christopher Columbus*

Christopher Columbus is probably the world's most famous explorer.  He believed

the world was round, and he was _____ to find a new and shorter

way to _____ the Indies.  He planned to do this by sailing west

from Europe.  No one had ever tried this before.

220

_____ Columbus couldn't get the money he needed for the trip. He asked the King of Portugal for help, but he said no.  Finally, Queen Isabella of Spain gave him the money.

In 1492, Columbus and his men sailed from Spain in three ships, the Niña, the Pinta, and the Santa Maria.  They were _____ of the problems and dangers of trying to cross the ocean in three small ships, but they were men of great

_____ .

They sailed for weeks without seeing land.  They began to lose hope and _____ if they would ever see land again.  The sailors wanted to go back to Spain, but Columbus got them to continue.

Then on October 12, 1492, one of the sailors saw a small island; this made them very happy.  They landed on the island, and Columbus named it San Salvador.  Their trip was a _____ .

Columbus thought that the island was part of the Indies. _____ , he called the Native Americans he met there Indians.

# Word List

The key words are listed in alphabetical order. The words derived from them are indented and immediately follow the key words.  The derived words are not in alphabetical order.

## A

accomplish 115
  accomplishment 121
advantage 125
  advantageous 132
  take advantage of 132
  disadvantage 132
afford 59
  affordable 65
afraid (of) 13
ago 115
aim 85
almost 23
a lot 13
a lot of 13
although 23
  though 25
amaze 153
  amazing 159
  amazement 159
apply 187
  application 194
  applicant 194
appointment 187
  appoint 194
approach 199
  approachable 206
argue 97
argument 97
around 3

ashamed 135
  shame 139
at first 209
at least 97
attempt 163
average 75
aware 187
  awareness 195

## B

bake 115
baker 115
bakery 115
be used to 115
bit 47
bite 13
bitter 97
  bitterly 104
  bitterness 104
blame 163
  blameless 170
borrow 59
both 37
bother 209
burn 37
  burner 43

## C

cautious 163
  caution 169
  cautiously 169
chase 198
cheer 153
  cheerful 160
  cheerfully 160
  cheerfulness 160
choose 59
  choice 66
courage 209
  courageous 216
  encourage 216
  encouragement 216
  discourage 216
  discouragement 216
crack 125
crash 163
crowd 153
  crowded 160

## D

damage 163
dangerous 173
  danger 179
  dangerously 179
deep 75
  deeply 81

pool 75
prefer 75
  preference 81
  preferable 81
protect 13
  protection 20
  protective 20
  protector 20
proud (of) 47
  proudly 54
  pride 54

## Q

quick 3
  quickly 9
  quickness 9
quit 97
quite 115

## R

rather 187
reach 199
recognize 199
  recognition 206
repair 125
reply 187
require 125
  requirement 132
right away 173
risk 209
  risky 216
rush 47

## S

score 153
search 125
shallow 75
share 37
shoot 85

shot 93
shout 97
skill 115
  skillful 121
  skillfully 121
slight 163
  slightly 170
so 125
spend 75
starve 23
  starvation 29
steal 199
still 37
storm 115
  stormy 121
stream 85
struggle 115
success 209
successful 209
  succeed 216
  unsuccessful 216
suddenly 163
  sudden 169
suggest 187
  suggestion 194
swallow 47

## T

therefore 187
thief 199
threaten 199
  threat 206
too 3
tough 209
trust 13
  trusting 20
try 23

## U

used to 173

## W

wake up 135
  awake 142
warn 173
warning 173
waste 3
  wasteful 9
weary 135
  weariness 141
weigh 23
weight 23
while (conjunction) 135
while (noun) 135
wipe 37
wonder 209
  wonderful 215
worry 173

# List of Key Words

**Chapter 1**
1. far
2. miss
3. too
4. have to
5. hurry
6. waste
7. quick
8. around

**Chapter 2**
1. a lot of
   a lot
2. afraid
3. own
4. protect
5. however
6. bite
7. trust
8. may

**Chapter 3**
1. only
2. weight
   weigh
3. lose
4. although
5. try
6. almost
7. starve
8. enjoy

**Chapter 4**
1. both
2. share
3. burn
4. still
5. improve
6. fun
7. wipe
8. hate

**Chapter 5**
1. proud
2. explore
3. fortunately
4. mistake
5. swallow
6. poison
7. rush
8. bit

**Chapter 6**
1. of course
2. expensive
3. neighbor
4. afford
5. choose
6. just
7. loan
8. borrow

**Chapter 7**
1. spend
2. average
3. prefer
4. pool
5. dive
6. deep
7. shallow
8. edge

**Chapter 8**
1. hunt
   hunter
2. shoot
3. stream
4. hesitate
5. aim
6. huge
7. lift
8. drag

**Chapter 9**
1. quit
2. at least
3. dull
4. earn
5. fool
   foolish
6. argue
   argument
7. shout
8. bitter

**Chapter 10**
1. ago
2. struggle
3. be used to
4. storm
5. skill
6. bake
   baker
   bakery
7. accomplish
8. quite

**Chapter 11**
1. enough
2. dream
3. search
4. crack
5. repair
6. advantage
7. so
8. require

**Chapter 12**
1. weary
2. fall asleep
3. hardly
4. while
5. pinch
6. wake up
7. shame
   ashamed
8. disturb

## Chapter 13
1. fan
2. amaze
3. discover
4. exciting
5. join
6. crowd
7. cheer
8. score

## Chapter 14
1. cautious
2. suddenly
3. crash
4. attempt
5. fault
6. blame
7. damage
8. slight

## Chapter 15
1. dangerous
2. main
3. warn
   warning
4. used to
5. pain
6. worry
7. right away
8. instead

## Chapter 16
1. therefore
2. appointment
3. apply
4. eager
5. rather
6. suggest
7. reply
8. aware

## Chapter 17
1. mild
2. approach
3. thief
4. threaten
5. steal
6. chase
7. reach
8. recognize

## Chapter 18
1. wonder
2. tough
3. bother
4. at first
5. partner
6. courage
7. risk
8. success
   successful